More Praise for
INSIDE VASUBANDHU'S YOGACARA

"Through Connelly's luminous teaching, some of Yogacara's most vivid and inspiring innovations come to
life. Newcomers and adherents to this lesser known
Buddhist school alike are lucky to have Connelly as an
exceptional guide to the central themes of Yogacara."

—*Publishers Weekly*, Starred Review

"Ben Connelly offers highly accessible commentary
on Vasubandhu's famous "Thirty Verses on Consciousness Only" in his new book *Inside Vasubandhu's
Yogacara*. Connelly's analysis is rich in doctrinal details
while keeping focused on the needs of contemporary
practitioners."

—*Lion's Roar*

INSIDE VASUBANDHU'S YOGACARA

A Practitioner's Guide

Ben Connelly

With a new translation from Sanskrit
by Ben Connelly and Weijen Teng

Foreword by Norman Fischer

Wisdom

Wisdom Publications
199 Elm Street
Somerville, MA 02144 USA
wisdompubs.org

Library of Congress Cataloging-in-Publication Data
Names: Connelly, Ben, author. | Vasubandhu.
  Triṃśikāvijñaptimātratāsiddhi. English.
Title: Inside Vasubandhu's Yogacara : a practitioner's guide / Ben Connelly.
Description: Somerville, MA : Wisdom Publications, 2016. | "With a new
  translation from Sanskrit by Ben Connelly and Weijen Teng." | Includes
  bibliographical references and index.
Identifiers: LCCN 2016008752 (print) | LCCN 2016042349 (ebook) | ISBN
  9781614292845 (paperback : alk. paper) | ISBN 1614292841 (paperback : alk.
  paper) | ISBN 9781614293088 (ebook) | ISBN 9781614293088 () | ISBN
  1614293082 ()
Subjects: LCSH: Vasubandhu. Triṃśikāvijñaptimātratāsiddhi. | Yogācāra
  (Buddhism) | BISAC: RELIGION / Buddhism / General (see also PHILOSOPHY /
  Buddhist). | RELIGION / Psychology of Religion. | RELIGION / Buddhism /
  Sacred Writings.
Classification: LCC BQ7529.V364 T7533 2016 (print) | LCC BQ7529.V364 (ebook)
  | DDC 294.3/92—dc23
LC record available at https://lccn.loc.gov/2016008752

ISBN 978-1-61429-284-5   ebook ISBN 978-1-61429-308-8

21 20 19 18
5 4 3 2

Cover design by Philip Pascuzzo.
Interior design by Gopa & Ted2, Inc.
Set in Requiem Text 10.9/15.8.

MIX
Paper from
responsible sources
FSC® C011935

Please visit fscus.org.

Contents

Foreword

BY NORMAN FISCHER

You have in your hands a wonderful book—a product of what I call Buddhism's "third wave."

I think of original Buddhism, in all its many manifestations in the many countries where it arose, as Buddhism's great "first wave." It rose up out of the deep waters of our first great cultures, when monarchs ruled the world in feudalistic agrarian societies, and writing was new. Developing in midst of such social arrangements, Buddhist teaching could not help but be influenced by them.

I call the initial encounter of this first Buddhism with contemporary thought and culture the "second wave." Its task was to be as faithful as possible to Buddhism's ancient wisdom while making it understandable and relevant in the new context. Historically, the second wave began in the mid-nineteenth century, with the West's "discovery" of Buddhism, and has continued more or less until the present.

And now we have a "third wave," represented by this book and its author. In this third wave, Buddhism is fairly well established as a spiritual practice everywhere in the contemporary world. The inevitable early exaggerations and cultural misunderstandings of Buddhism's adoption into the West having been more or less overcome, Westerners like Ben Connelly can now train in Buddhism steadily for decades under Western teachers with a lifetime of experience in the practice. For teachers like Ben, Buddhism is more natural and normal than it was for people of my generation. When I began Buddhist practice in the late 1960s there were almost no Western Dharma centers. It took me a few years to hear of the San Francisco Zen Center, then newly formed as the first major Buddhist center in the West. By the time Ben began his practice, Zen and other Buddhist centers had been long established all over the country.

Naturally, the literature produced by these three waves of Buddhism differs. The first wave gave us the primary ancient texts that have survived through the generations. The second wave needed good translations of primary sources, initial introductory texts by the great Asian teachers who first transmitted the teachings, and informal interpretations by the first Western teachers trying to find a new voice for this ancient wisdom. The third wave, just beginning, is now giving us wonderful books like *Inside Vasubandhu's Yogacara*—contemporary Western commentaries to traditional texts, grounded in solid practice.

We are past the moment of being introduced to and amazed by this great teaching. Now we are ready to learn how to make use of it for the lives we are living here in our time.

A key aspect of this third wave is that it arises with—or perhaps has given rise to—the mindfulness movement, a secular approach to Buddhism grounded in mindfulness meditation and associated practices. Aligned with contemporary Western psychology and, especially, with a range of research on cognitive processes, mindfulness has had a profound impact on how Buddhism is understood in the modern world—and how the modern world understands itself. While first-wave Buddhism was clearly an Asian religion, third-wave Buddhism erases the boundary between religion and spirituality, faith and praxis, East and West. For most Buddhists today, practice has to do with how we live, how we train our minds and hearts, how we, in Ben's phrase "take care of our consciousness."

Third-wave Buddhist teachers like Ben stand on the shoulders of their predecessors. They have a solid understanding of the traditional teachings, but they do not simply take them as is. They ask of them, what works? What can be useful and practical for the contemporary practitioner? They assume, as this book does, that the teachings are already ours and that it is up to us to find out how to apply them.

Vasubandhu's "Thirty Verses" is a famous text,

important for more than seventeen hundred years. When I first looked at early attempts at translation and commentary, I was immensely impressed—and intimidated. I could barely understand it. So I am frankly amazed by Ben's daring and skill to undertake this project so successfully. He and his learned colleague Weijen Teng have made a new, clear translation of the Sanskrit text, and Ben has provided a straightforward and eminently useful commentary.

Yogacara thought is subtle and hard to fully appreciate. And yet, as the Buddha himself noted, we are all philosophers, full of dysfunctional ideas about reality. So it is in our best interests to examine these ideas and disabuse ourselves of the worst of them. In this book Ben manages not only to explain Yogacara thinking, but to show how it fits into the edifice of Buddhism—and, most importantly of all, demonstrate its relevance for the contemporary practitioner who is concerned to be mindful and humane in her living.

How, I wonder, can Ben accomplish such a difficult task? Maybe it's because he is a musician. As a person who likes to read philosophical texts, I have noticed that there is music to meaning. When you begin to hear the song behind the words, the words become clear. This, it seems to me, is the magic that Ben has wrought in his book: he's heard Vasubandhu's song and has sung it for us, in our own idiom and situation.

I feel very fortunate to be around for this new wave

of Buddhism, to be able to learn and benefit from it. And I am grateful for this book, and for the friendship of its marvelous author.

Introduction

Thank you for joining me in this opportunity to engage with the Way, to engage with an opportunity, available in each moment, to offer our attention and effort to peace, wellness, and harmony.

I am writing this so that we can bring some old and beautiful wisdom to life, so that together we can celebrate and take up the most concise and practical text of one of the most revered and influential figures in Buddhist history. Vasubandhu showed his compassion and appreciation for us through a lifetime of devotion to the path of freedom and well-being for all, and we have this chance to give this love and appreciation right back with our own investigation and practice. Yogacara teachings may seem hard to understand at first, but by being with them together we can see that they show a comprehensive and powerful model for how to devote our lives to universal well-being.

In this book, I'll spend a minimum of time digging into the many and fascinating philosophical implications of Vasubandhu's Yogacara; instead, I'll devote my energy to showing how it can provide a template for compassionate engagement with what is here right now. Together, we can be empowered by these teachings to dive joyfully and kindly into life.

WHO WAS VASUBANDHU?

We don't know much about Vasubandhu, but there are some aspects of his story that are widely circulated and probably have some relation to the actual events.

The records we have date Vasubandhu's life to the fourth century. He was born to a brahmin family in India and became one of the most revered teachers of Abhidharma, which systematizes and analyzes the earliest Buddhist teachings. Later in life, he became a devotee of Mahayana, with the help of his half-brother Asanga, the other great genius of Yogacara. Vasubandhu's ability to integrate his extraordinary understanding of both Abhidharma and Mahayana thought and practice, and to express them in his numerous writings, helped give birth to the new tradition of Yogacara. This book is a commentary on Vasubandhu's most practice-oriented text, "Thirty Verses on Consciousness Only," which succinctly expresses the central themes of Yogacara.

He is included in all Zen lineages in China and Japan, and is revered and quoted in texts from many other Tibetan, East Asian, and Indian schools of Buddhism. In the Soto Zen tradition, Vasubandhu's importance is expressed during the ancient ritual of chanting the eighty names of the ancestral lineage, dating back to the Buddha. As the community intones the names amid the candle glow and drifting incense, the head teacher does deep, full bows at the names of the six most influential figures in the Soto tradition: Buddha, Nagarjuna, Vasubandhu, Bodhidharma, Huineng, and Dogen Zenji.

WHAT IS YOGACARA?

Yogacara means "yoga practice." *Yoga* is a word that has come to mean bending and stretching to many Americans but, in its original sense, refers to joining together or uniting. Yogacara, therefore, is about integration, connection, and harmony. Yoga practice traditionally includes ethical living, meditative absorption and analysis, and training of breath and body. Yogacara teachings in particular emphasize compassionate living and meditation.

The Yogacara tradition is traced to the appearance of the *Samdhinirmocana Sutra* around the third century CE, then through the many writings of Vasubandhu and Asanga, to the *Lankavatara Sutra*'s appearance, and the transmission of these texts from India into Tibet and China in the middle of the first millennium. Although no longer extant as a distinct school of practice, Yogacara continues to have a strong influence in Mahayana Buddhism. For instance, Yogacara study has historically been and often still is included in Tibetan monastic training. Xuanzang, who is mythologized in the popular Chinese legend *Journey to the West*, composed as his magnum opus the *Chengweishilun*, a translation and commentary on the "Thirty Verses" that has exerted a major influence on Chinese Buddhism. Yogacara was also central to the birth of Zen; Zen's founder Bodhidharma reportedly referred to the *Lankavatara Sutra*, a Yogacara text, as the "only" sutra, and early Zen texts are larded with Yogacara terms.

Yogacara arose as an attempt to integrate the most powerful aspects of the earliest Buddhist teachings and later Mahayana teachings. There was growing sectarian argumentation between the proponents of these two bodies of teaching, and Yogacara sought to show how the teachings were not actually in conflict and to allow for practitioners to access the profound transformative benefits of both traditions. Yogacara provides a beautiful model for how to work with the great range of Buddhist traditions that have arrived in the West from all over Asia in the last fifty years.

THREE SCHOOLS OF BUDDHISM

Throughout this book I will refer to three bodies of Buddhist teaching relevant to the development of Yogacara: Early Buddhism, Abhidharma, and Mahayana.

Early Buddhism refers to the very first tradition of

Buddhism and to the teachings that can be found in the Pali Canon, the earliest substantial body of Buddhist teachings available to us. Since these were first written down several hundred years after the death of the historical Buddha, Siddhartha Gautama, it is hard to know how accurately they reflect his teachings. However, they are probably as close as we can get. These teachings lay out a path of practice for going from suffering to non-suffering, from samsara to nirvana. They are held up as most valuable by the modern Theravada and Vipassana traditions.

Abhidharma means something like "about Dharma," or "meta-Dharma." The Early Buddhist records we have in the Pali Canon contain a very large section called the abhidharma, which organizes elements of other teachings into lists. There are thousands of lists, and lists of lists. It is a rather dizzying body of literature. However when I use the term Abhidharma, I refer not to the Pali abhidharma but to a closely related later textual tradition. At the dawn of the first millennium, the Abhidharma movement sought to work with these lists and all the other existing teachings and refine and systemize them. Because the Early Buddhist teachings were compiled over the Buddha's forty-year teaching career and then passed down orally for a few hundred years, they did not always logically hang together; Abhidharmists sought to create a more complete coherence from this great mass of earlier teachings. Abhidharma teachings are notoriously and incredibly complex. They are a phenomenally detailed cataloguing of the process of consciousness. This is the tradition in which Vasubandhu was originally trained.

Mahayana, or "Great Vehicle," Buddhism arose at the start of the first millennium as well, but it took a radical turn. Rooting its thought and practice in a small body of Early Buddhist teachings, it put an enormous emphasis on nondualism, often described as emptiness or interdependence. Over and over again Mahayana sutras point out that everything we think or believe is rooted in dualistic thought, and thus none of it is ultimately real, and all of it leaves us in a web of our mind's making. We may say there is day and night, but these are not actually separate phenomena. They are interdependent, empty of separation, not-two. You can't have day without night; they interdependently are. Absolutely everything that can be conceived or spoken is like this. Mahayana teaches that what you think or believe something to be is conventionally useful but not the absolute truth, and that seeing connection, rather than separation, is the ground of compassionate freedom of mind. Mahayana teachings often suggest that the dualisms of Early Buddhism and the categorizations of Abhidharma are a distraction from realizing liberation right now through unconceptualized nondualism. In general the Early Buddhist schools' emphasis on the path of personal liberation and attainment of nirvana, and the Mahayana idealization of the bodhi-sattva's path of devotion to universal enlightenment, were often seen as in direct contradiction.

During Vasubandhu's time and still today, we find great debate about which view is correct, which is best. Vasubandhu's "Thirty Verses" finds a way to make these differing ideas harmonize in practice. The verses show how differing points of view and practices can help us to be free, at peace, and available to give our best to the world. They are the work of someone who, instead of picking sides, poured his genius and effort into helping people come together. They show a way that finds common ground but also honors difference. They help us to access the best of both Early Buddhist and Mahayana thought in our own lives and practices.

A TWOFOLD MODEL OF UNDERSTANDING

The "Thirty Verses" focuses on a twofold model of practice and understanding—the study of the functioning of consciousness and the study of the nature of phenomena—although ultimately it suggests that these two are not separate.

For the first, it uses a model of experience called the *eight consciousnesses* and teaches us how to practice with and understand consciousness to liberate ourselves from afflictive emotions like anger, selfishness, and laziness. This set of teachings is closely tied to Early Buddhism and has extraordinary transformative psychological power.

For the study of the nature of phenomena, it uses what is called the *three-natures model*, which is rooted in Mahayana teachings that emphasize letting go of delusion, letting go of the way of seeing that creates alienation: the delusion that our happiness or suffering are dependent on the slings and arrows of an external world from which we are separate. The three-natures teachings help us to realize the totality of our connection and intimacy with everything.

Yogacarins often speak of two barriers: the barrier of afflictive emotion and the barrier of delusion. The first half of "Thirty Verses" uses the eight-consciousnesses model to treat the barrier of afflictive emotion, and the second half uses the three natures to take care of the barrier of delusion. The "Thirty Verses" is about empowering us to see that we are victims of neither our own karma (habits of emotion, thought, and action) nor apparently external phenomena.

CONSCIOUSNESS ONLY BUDDHISM

The "Thirty Verses" is one of the most concise and accessible expressions of what is often called Consciousness Only Buddhism. This refers to a movement that began in first-century India, grew in prevalence for several hundred years, and then left traces throughout two thousand years of subsequent Buddhist thought. It is closely related to, but not synonymous with, the Yogacara tradition. Sometimes called *mind-only* and generally appearing in Sanskrit as *cittamatra*, it carries an array of meanings. The ideas embedded in this phrase are rooted in the earliest Buddhist teachings and became formative concepts in Tibetan, East Asian, and subsequently the nascent American Buddhism.

Consciousness Only alludes to the idea that, in Buddhist practice, we have one principal concern: taking care of our consciousness. This draws us away from the conventional tendency to spend our lives trying to grasp and control apparently external things. It points to the fact that whatever we experience is mediated by consciousness, or as the first line of the *Dhammapada* says, "Our life is shaped by our mind." It presents the view that ultimately we do not know what is "out there" in the apparently external world. We only know that we have this moment of conscious experience.

Here is a reflection of Consciousness Only in a classic Zen koan:

Two monks were debating outside the monastery. One said to the other, "The wind is moving." The other said, "The flag is moving."

Sixth ancestor Huineng was walking by and said,
"Not the wind, not the flag: mind is moving."

This school of thought puts a great deal of emphasis—more than other Buddhist systems—on the concept that the main source of suffering in our lives is our sense that we are a "self" experiencing "other" things. It invites us to realize that this moment of consciousness is instead Consciousness Only, with no self separate from anything else. Consciousness Only is occasionally translated as "mere consciousness," or "merely consciousness," to remind us that whatever it is about which we're becoming agitated, irritated, overjoyed, overwhelmed, or aggrieved is just consciousness—not a real thing, but a projection of mental tendencies. It's not such a big deal. We can take care of what's here with some lightness, some compassion, and be well.

It might appear that such a teaching denies or draws us away from the possibility of service to others and a life devoted to the well-being of the world, which is the heart of Mahayana Buddhism, but as we will see, Consciousness Only is in harmony with both the Early Buddhist and the Mahayanist school of thought, a way of seeing and living that is about promoting complete peace and harmony.

Here is a story from the Theravadan tradition with a Consciousness Only flavor, about Voramai Kabilsingh, the first Thai woman to receive full ordination and take the accompanying 311 precepts:

> A young man asked, "How do you keep the 311 precepts?"
> Voramai Kabilsingh responded, "I keep only one precept."
> Surprised, the young man asked, "What is that?"
> She answered, "I just watch my mind."

It is important to note that the idea of Consciousness Only is not geared toward explaining the nature of reality or the universe but toward explaining experience, the material we have to work with in terms of taking care of human suffering. In philosophical terms, rather than a teaching about metaphysics, this is a teaching that relates to epistemology, the nature of knowing, and soteriology, the way to freedom, wellness, and enlightenment. This tradition does not claim that the universe is made of consciousness or that there is nothing but consciousness. It simply tells us we don't know anything that is not mediated by consciousness; thus, working with the way our consciousness operates is the best way to promote wellness and nonsuffering.

Although this idea that there is not a "self" experiencing "other" things—there is only consciousness—existed in many Buddhist schools before Yogacara

came along, none of them held this up as so fundamental. This teaching has taken deep roots in Buddhist thought throughout Asia and America, so much
so that many people I know, who have never heard of
Consciousness Only or Yogacara, assume that this has
always been the very heart of Buddhist teaching.

CONSCIOUSNESS ONLY AND NONSELF

Sometimes people claim that Consciousness Only
contradicts the central Buddhist tenet that all things
are empty of an independent, lasting self. They cri-
tique it by saying it turns the Buddhist path of seeing
through selfhood and letting it go into one of making
a perfect self. Similarly many Western philosophers
refer to Consciousness Only as *idealism*, or a philosophical system in which the only thing that exists is mind.

Although there are some Consciousness Only teachings that do seem to teach this, the "Thirty Verses" does
not. Most teachings from this tradition do not claim
that *ultimately* only mind exists, nor that it is a lasting
self or soul, and many of them specifically warn against
misconstruing them in this way. The "Thirty Verses"
is particularly careful to avoid this potentially self-
absorbed trap. Xuanzang writes in the *Chengweishilun*, a
commentary on the "Thirty Verses" and the most influential Yogacara text in East Asia, "In order to refute the
false attachment to a really existing realm outside the

mind and its activities, we teach Consciousness Only, but if one believes that Consciousness Only really exists, this is no different from attachment to external objects, and it remains attachment to phenomena." Throughout Consciousness Only texts, including the "Thirty Verses," we find similar reminders that, like all Buddhist discourse, these are provisional teachings, whose purpose is to promote the alleviation of suffering through letting go of attachment. They are not a means of explaining the universe; they are just words that can help us seek freedom.

But all this talk is Consciousness Only, or merely consciousness. Let's not get too wrapped up in it. The words emerging on this white space as I type, and the unwilled, unknown subtle motion of your eyes across the page as you read, are part of a vast unfolding that we can never fully comprehend. All the ideas laid forth in the book, every birdsong that you hear, and every moment of bickering with your boss, or worrying about your children, every moment of calm, open stillness as you move mindfully through your day—let's not get too caught up in them, but let them be and let them go; they're only consciousness.

CONSCIOUSNESS ONLY IN PRACTICE

We can see the roots of Consciousness Only in the earliest Buddhist teachings. The Buddha's first teaching was the Eightfold Path, which he laid out and referred to throughout his life as his Way to alleviation of suffering. Buddhism is the promotion of well-being, and the Eightfold Path is how you do it. If we look at the steps on the path—right view, intention, speech, action, livelihood, effort, mindfulness, and concentration—we can see that there is nothing in it that is external to our own mind and actions. This doesn't mean that things external to our own choices don't affect well-being; it just means that since we don't have control of them, they are not the concern of the way of practice Buddha recommends for our wellness. This path radically directs us to concentrate on our own choices, our own actions, and our own minds, which is in direct contradiction to most of our habitual tendencies.

Let's imagine it's December and you have a few packages to mail, gifts for nieces and nephews perhaps. On the way to work you stop at the post office. The line is very long. You glance at your watch fearing you'll be late. The people in line are tense, they shuffle about, inching forward. "Why don't they have more workers at the desk?" You fume in frustration. It does not smell good in here. Shuffling forward, you realize that it is taking five minutes for the woman at one desk to figure out how to mail her package. Come on! How hard is it? A child in front is involved in a tense exchange with her mother. Perhaps you have some great ideas about how this mother could be a better parent. Sweat beads on your forehead as you glance at the clock yet again and tensely check the messages on your phone. The line inches forward . . .

Alternately, upon entering the line, if you focus on consciousness itself, you might notice the frustration appear in your mind, be intimate with the tense feelings in the body, be aware of the judgmental thoughts floating into being and disappearing. You might realize the intimacy of your mind's suffering with that of everyone in the room, with that of all the people in the world. You might see through your own suffering and into your profound connection, and you might relax and pass out some quiet smiles and kind words as you move through the line . . . and, of course, still get to work late. Directing the attention to consciousness itself does not create a world according to our desires, but it is the happier way both for you and for others.

THE "THIRTY VERSES" IN PRACTICE

The "Thirty Verses," like much classical Buddhist literature, is challenging. Do not be surprised if, on the first reading, these verses seem opaque. This book is a guide to make them accessible to your own heart, mind, and practice. According to some old texts, there were ten commentaries on the "Thirty Verses" written near the time of its creation, and each of these presented distinct views. Most of these are no longer extant. In the last fifty years, we have seen varying interpretations of this work as well. My book is not an attempt to create an absolutely true and definitive explanation of the meaning of Vasubandhu's work, nor will I spend much time analyzing the distinctions between various others' explanations. This book forwards the most practical implications of these verses and lays them out in a way that you may take them into your life.

The "Thirty Verses" reveals a fourfold model of how to offer our effort: being aware of the tremendous power of our cognitive and emotional habits, practicing mindfulness of our body and emotional states, being aware of the interdependence of all things, and practicing meditation with no object. In simplest terms, we could say this is about learning to be intimate with both ourselves and everything, so that we may be compassionate, joyous, and free. This model of practice allows us to shed harmful emotional states and realize the completeness of our connection to each thing. We can learn to meet the surly, disheveled man on the street without fear or judgment; to meet a frustrated and exhausted spouse with kind, wholehearted listening; to meet our own aching heart with warm, loving attention; to meet our suffering planet with changes in how we consume; to not even really meet anything, but realize we are all already completely part of one unknowable wholeness, to be the stillness of a lake unbroken by the ripples of a fallen raindrop.

One of the most helpful things one can do is to make a commitment to a simple meditation practice and to act with compassion. Everything written in this book is rooted in and arises from meditative experience and is designed to help us cultivate the peace and harmony found in devoting oneself to seeing things as they are while engaging in kind action. Although the "Thirty Verses" contains much wisdom on how to be in the world, its wisdom only really flowers if paired with a commitment to meditation practice and beneficial living. I heartily pray that my effort in writing this book, and your effort in engaging with these teachings, may carry forward both Vasubandhu's vision for how to give ourselves to the well-being of the world and the central intention of all Buddhist teaching: the alleviation of suffering.

In America today we are creating new and distinct forms of Buddhism informed by the many strains of Asian Buddhist and yogic thought that have come to our shores. In fourth-century India as well, there was a great diversity of practices and ideas. In that time Vasubandhu, as part of the Yogacara movement, sought at the end of his life to reconcile these many systems and demonstrate how they could be effectively integrated into a single system of practice. His "Thirty Verses" is his most concise, comprehensive, and accessible work. This work shows a way toward honoring and employing the whole of the Buddhist tradition including Tibetan and Zen Buddhism, which were profoundly influenced by Yogacara ideas. It lays out a path of practice that integrates the most potent of Buddhism's possibilities: Early Buddhism's emphasis on shedding afflictive emotions and impulses and the Mahayana emphasis on shedding divisive concepts; the path of individual liberation and the path of freeing all beings; the path to nirvana and the path of enlightenment as the very ground of being right now.

Although Yogacara has a reputation for being extremely complex, the "Thirty Verses" distills the principles of these traditions to their most practical forms, and this book follows that sense of focus; it avoids difficult and abstruse byways and goes to the heart of the matter—how do we alleviate suffering through shedding our emotional knots and our sense of alienation?

As a Zen priest I have chanted these verses countless times, ever since I learned that Thich Nhat Hanh and his fellow monks were required to memorize them as part of their training. I have devoted myself to studying and practicing their wisdom. Although my training is as a Zen priest I know these verses have enormous value for the many types of Buddhists across the globe. This book is for others who are interested in bringing the breadth of Buddhist wisdom into a single way of practice.

Thirty Verses
on Consciousness Only

Vasubandhu

Translated by Ben Connelly and Weijen Teng

Everything conceived as self or other occurs in the
transformation of consciousness. || 1 ||

This transformation has three aspects:
The ripening of karma, the consciousness of a self,
and the imagery of sense objects. || 2 ||

The first of these is also called *alaya*, the store
consciousness, which contains all karmic seeds.
What it holds and its perception of location are
unknown. || 3 ||

It is always associated with sense-contact, attention,
sensation, perception, and volition,
Neither pleasant nor unpleasant. It is unobstructed,
and karmically neutral,
Like a river flowing. In enlightenment it is overturned
at its root. || 4 ||

Dependent on the store consciousness and taking it as
    its object,
Manas, the consciousness of a self, arises, which consists
    of thinking. || 5 ||

It is always associated with four afflictions, self-view,
    self-delusion, self-pride, and self-love,
And is obstructed, but karmically neutral. Along with
    these four, || 6 ||

From where it is born come sense-contact, attention,
    sensation, perception, and volition.
It is not found in enlightenment, the meditation of
    cessation, or the supramundane path. || 7 ||

That is the second transformation, the third is the
    perception of the six senses,
Which are beneficial, harmful, or neither. || 8 ||

It is associated with three kinds of mental factors:
    universal, specific, and beneficial,
As well as the afflictions and secondary afflictions,
    and the three sensations. || 9 ||

The universal factors are sense-contact, attention,
    sensation, perception, and volition.
The specific are aspiration, resolve, memory,
    concentration, and intellection. || 10 ||

The beneficial factors are faith, conscience, humility,
    lack of desire, aversion, and delusion,
Energy, tranquility, carefulness, equanimity, and
    nonviolence. || 11 ||

The afflictions are desire, aversion, delusion, pride,
    wrong view, and doubt.
The secondary afflictions are anger, hatred, hypocrisy,
    malice, envy, selfishness, || 12 ||

Deceitfulness, guile, arrogance, harmfulness, lack of
    conscience and humility, sluggishness,
Restlessness, lack of faith, laziness, carelessness,
    forgetfulness, distraction, and unawareness. || 13 ||

Remorse, sleepiness, initial thought, and analysis can
    be either afflictive or not. || 14 ||

The five sense consciousnesses arise on the root
    consciousness together or separately,
Depending on conditions, like waves arise on water. || 15 ||

Thought consciousness always manifests except in
    the realm of no thought,
The two thought-free meditation states,
    unconsciousness, and thought-free sleep. || 16 ||

This transformation of consciousness is
conceptualization,
What is conceptualized does not exist, thus everything
is projection only. || 17 ||

Consciousness is all the seeds transforming in various
ways
Through mutual influence producing the many
conceptualizations. || 18 ||

Karmic impressions and the impressions of grasping self
and other
Produce further ripening as the former karmic effect
is exhausted. || 19 ||

Whatever thing is conceptualized by whatever
conceptualization
Is of an imaginary nature; it does not exist. || 20 ||

The other-dependent nature is a conceptualization
arising from conditions;
The complete, realized nature is the other-dependent
nature's always being devoid of the imaginary. || 21 ||

Thus it is neither the same nor different from the
other-dependent;
Like impermanence, etc., when one isn't seen, the other
also is not seen. || 22 ||

With the threefold nature is a threefold absence of
    self-nature,
So it has been taught that all things have no self. || 23 ||

The imaginary is without self by definition. The other-
    dependent does not exist by itself.
The third is no-self nature—that is, || 24 ||

The complete, realized nature of all phenomena, which
    is thusness—
Since it is always already thus, projection only. || 25 ||

As long as consciousness does not rest in projection only,
The tendencies of grasping self and other will not
    cease. || 26 ||

By conceiving what you put before you to be projection
    only,
You do not rest in just this. || 27 ||

When consciousness does not perceive any object, then
    it rests in projection only;
When there is nothing to grasp, there is no grasping. || 28 ||

Without thought, without conception, this is the
    supramundane awareness:
The overturning of the root, the ending of the two
    barriers. || 29 ||

It is the inconceivable, wholesome, unstained, constant realm,

The blissful body of liberation, the Dharma body of the great sage. || 30 ||

1
Self and Other

Everything conceived as self or other occurs
in the transformation of consciousness. || 1 ||

I invite you to take a moment to investigate what you
are experiencing right now. In all likelihood, you have
a sense of being in a location, perhaps in a chair or a
bed. There are sensations in a body that you think
of as yours, there is a visual field that can be scanned
from left to right (that is to say, from what you probably think of as your left and right), there are things
behind you that you cannot see but you can feel: the
soft back of a chair perhaps. There are words in front
of you that you conceive to be my words that you
would likely say that you are reading. We can divide
everything in this moment of experience into things
that we conceive to be ourselves and things that we
conceive to be other than ourselves, with ourselves
unconsciously placed in the center. Whether we
know it or not, this division and this self-centering
is constantly occurring, and this division—and the
problems it causes and the possibility of transcending

them through intimacy with them—is the principal subject of the "Thirty Verses."

A brief investigation of our consciousness like the one above is likely to lead us to the idea that we have a consciousness that experiences things: consciousness is the self, and the world around us is other. At the start of this work, Vasubandhu points toward another view: "Everything conceived as self or other occurs in the transformation of consciousness." Neither the self nor the other is consciousness; they are merely conceptions occurring within a process of consciousness.

The transformation of consciousness is a constant flow. If you look at experience there are not fixed elements or even moments; there is simply a process, a transformation. The first thing these verses give us is an opportunity to experience a sense of wonder about what we are experiencing right now, a sense that our most basic understanding of where and what we are in the world is not quite right, that we are instead involved in a mysterious, flowing unfolding. We see this teaching reflected in the Tibetan classic *The Thirty-Seven Practices of the Bodhisattva* by Tokme Zangpo (1245–1369):

Whatever arises in experience is your own mind.
Mind itself is free of any conceptual limitations.
Know that and don't generate self-other
    fixations—
this is the practice of a bodhisattva.

Consciousness Only puts forth the split between subject and object as the ultimate aspect of our consciousness we must see through if we want to realize our capacity to appear in the world in a purely kind and joyful way. As we will see at the end of the "Thirty Verses," letting go of the sense that we are a self experiencing things is the way to enter this mysterious flowing unfolding, so that whatever is here that we might call *ourselves* is just a natural, generous, joyful, compassionate occurrence. The Buddha called himself *tathagata* or "that which is thus coming and going." He described himself as merely a flowing occurrence, and the outward form that took was constant, calm, compassionate availability to people who came to him for help. This is the way of being these verses offer to you.

In Sanskrit the first two words of this text are *atma* and *dharma*. *Atma* is a key Indian term meaning "self" or "soul." *Dharma* means various things, but here it means "phenomenon," something that is experienced, something other than ourself. Many Early Buddhist practices involved investigating phenomena and realizing that they were not one's self: for example, seeing that one's thoughts are not one's self, the sensations in the body are not one's self, feelings are not one's self, etc. By seeing that all these things are not our selves we become liberated from the endless cycle of dissatisfaction that characterizes human experience. We see that that there is no *I* to be dissatisfied. We can let go of clinging, let go of feeling upset over and over again because the world does not function according to our desires.

These practices were developed over the years, and great bodies of literature and practice grew around them: the Abhidharma. The Abhidharma view came to be that although atman didn't exist, dharmas did. Abhidharmists refined a complex system of categorization of dharmas that were to be seen and memorized. Deep practice was to see the constant flow of phenomena, of dharmas, without having a sense of one's self in the midst of it. As the great fifth-century Theravada monk Buddhaghosa wrote:

> There is suffering, but none who suffers;
> Doing exists although there is no doer;

At some point, Mahayana Buddhists started to think that the Abhidharmists had gotten stuck. Stuck on their investigation of dharmas. Stuck on memorizing, categorizing, and believing in their system. Great bodies of Mahayana literature sprang up teaching that dharmas were empty of self-existence. As it says at the beginning of the most widely chanted and celebrated Mahayana text, the *Heart Sutra*, the bodhisattva of compassion, Avalokiteshvara, relieves all suffering by seeing that all dharmas, all phenomena, are empty, without their own self-nature. Deep practice in the

Mahayana tradition was to see that nothing at all had its own self-nature. So in the early part of the first millennium, there were great debates about whose view or method was correct, or most helpful.

Yogacara, in general, sought to reconcile divisions in Buddhist thought. And here Vasubandhu, using Consciousness Only teachings, pursues that end. He says that whatever conceptions one has about self and other occur in the transformation of consciousness, they are all Consciousness Only. That is to say, within this transformation of consciousness, one can realize that no phenomena is our self, as the Abhidharmists say, and one can also realize that phenomena are not themselves, that they are empty of an independent, lasting nature. This verse gives us a ground on which to do our practice, including the practice of realizing that there is no ground. This ground is this ineffable transformation of consciousness far beyond any conceptions we may have of what it is—it is just this moment of experience.

It seems clear that Vasubandhu hoped to bring people together with these verses and to reconcile systems of thought, but his interest was not academic. He reconciles these two systems of thought because they are both valuable for helping people find peace, compassion, and kind action. The Abhidharma system of dharmas, as we will see in verses 10–14, focuses on whether the mind contains beneficial or afflictive emotions and provides a method for cultivating the beneficial ones and letting go of the afflictive ones, so that we may be profound peace and kindness. Its psychological precision helps us to know and let go of harmful habits, even those of which we are usually unaware. The Mahayana emphasis on emptiness of all phenomena can allow us to be completely liberated from the delusion of separateness, our constantly arising tendency to put ourselves at the center, so that we may be vast freedom and compassion. Yogacara teachings, including the "Thirty Verses," refer to two barriers: afflictive emotion and delusion. The Abhidharma teachings and practices in the first half of this book are to help you let go of afflictions; the Mahayana-style teachings in the second half are to help you let go of delusion. The vision of the "Thirty Verses" is that both of these methods combined are more powerful than either alone, and they can provide anyone willing to do the practice a way to shed suffering and step into a life of ease, joy, and compassionate action.

2

The Eight-Consciousnesses Model

This transformation has three aspects:

The ripening of karma, the consciousness of a self,
and the imagery of sense objects. || 2 ||

This verse introduces us to the main subject of the first fifteen verses of this work: the Yogacara model for understanding consciousness. The purpose of this model is to help us see how we can let go of tendencies that lead to afflictive, painful, and difficult emotions and cultivate the capacity to manifest beneficial ones: emotions that are both more pleasant to experience and conducive to kindness toward others. This verse begins to explain the eight-consciousnesses model, a Yogacara innovation that is an expansion of Early Buddhism's teaching of the six consciousnesses, sometimes called the All.

In the earliest Buddhist teachings, Buddha says that to be free from suffering it's necessary to understand the All, which is comprised of these six consciousnesses: sight, sound, smell, taste, touch, and thought. This All is the totality of our momentary conscious experience. We are instructed to direct our attention toward and directly know these six consciousnesses. The point is not that we develop some theory or ideas about them; rather, we should know them intimately, in a way that is much deeper than words can describe and that is suffused with compassion. In Buddhist practice we come to know things through mindfulness, through nonjudgmental, moment-to-moment awareness. As we pay attention to sight, sound, smell, taste, touch, and thoughts, we begin to see that they are just things that come and go. We begin to dis-identify with them, to not hold tightly but let them be. The realization that our thoughts are just something that is coming and going, that they are not ourselves, is often one of the most striking and liberating aspects people experience when they begin meditation.

This All is what this verse describes as "the imagery of sense objects." When Vasubandhu says that there are three aspects of the transformation of consciousness, these six together make up the third of these transformations.

We call them *transformations* because they are just coming and going; they are simply a process of endless change. And *imagery* literally means the language used in literature to paint a vivid sensory picture in order to elicit emotion. This is a somewhat free translation of the Sanskrit term *vijñapti*, which is key to the last half of the "Thirty Verses" and will be discussed in detail later in the book. The purpose of its use here is to point out that what we take to be reality, the basic data of our sense experience, is actually in large part a creation of the habits of our consciousness, or we might say a manifestation of our unconscious narratives, and is intimately connected to the way we experience emotions.

So, this third transformation, the imagery of sense objects, is a process we know as *experience*: the All is readily apparent to us. Right now you can see this text, you are experiencing thought and sensations in the body, as a result of the six consciousnesses.

The first transformation, described in this verse as "the ripening of karma," and the second, "the consciousness of a self," are referred to in Sanskrit as *alaya-vijnana*, or store consciousness, and *manas*, respectively. These are the two elements that Yogacara added to its model of consciousnesses: your past conditioning and your sense that there is a "you" that is experiencing things.

The store consciousness is a way to describe the process by which karma ripens. The conditioning of our past is depicted as karmic seeds and the way those manifest in our present-moment experience as karmic fruit. Have you ever been standing in the rain and seen one person shuffling along scowling at the clouds and another smiling and bouncing along in the downpour? The emotional reactions and conduct of the two people is the result of their karmic conditioning. Karma doesn't make rain; it makes smiles and frowns, it makes hugs and fists.

THE EIGHT CONSCIOUSNESSES			
		8	*Alaya*, or store consciousness: "the ripening of karma"
		7	*Manas*: "consciousness of self"
The All: "imagery of sense objects"		6	Mind/thought
		5	Sight
		4	Sound
		3	Smell
		2	Taste
		1	Touch

The manas consciousness creates the sense that there is a self that experiences objects. In meditation as the storytelling mind relaxes and we settle into the coming and going of phenomena—the crying of gulls, the occasional sighs of the meditator next to us, the worrying about how soon the bell will ring—we often notice that there is a persistent aspect of mind that is a sense of experiencing things. In the Early Buddhist teachings, one meditation adept called this "the residual conceit: 'I am.'" Katagiri Roshi called it "the observer" and said that this is one of the hardest things to let go of in meditation. This is manas, the sense that there is an *I* experiencing things.

Here we set the stage for our investigation of consciousness, so that we can be intimate with it, so that we may understand how to help it be well. The first half of the "Thirty Verses" will deal with the store consciousness, manas, and the six senses. We will see how by mindfulness of what appears in or as the six senses, we can experience and let go of the seeds of suffering in the storehouse, and plant and cultivate beneficial seeds. In so doing, we can participate in this transformation of consciousness, rather than being unconsciously swept along with it. We can offer our effort to allowing this process to be one that is conducive to well-being. We can see that the beneficial states of mind are ones where we are kind and compassionate toward whatever or whoever is here in the present moment. We can see how that softens and erodes our sense that we are self, separate from anything else. We can realize the Buddhist promise of our ability to joyfully disappear into the pure harmonious dynamic activity of the moment—consciousness only.

3

Store Consciousness

The first of these is also called *alaya*,
the store consciousness, which contains
all karmic seeds.

What it holds and its
perception of location are unknown. || 3 ||

The store consciousness is a way of describing how past conditions come together to form our present experience. We can think of it as an unconscious aspect of our life that colors and is the basis for that of which we are conscious. It is where all the impressions of the past, our karmic seeds, are constantly involved in a process of transformation that our mind believes to be reality.

The concept of this aspect of consciousness is a model for understanding why we act the way we do, but most importantly it addresses the issue of how we can transform or let go of afflictive emotions. As we will see in later chapters, we can cultivate karmic seeds that are conducive to happiness and kindness through mindfulness and a gentle approach to letting go of harmful tendencies. Thus we can transform the contents of the storehouse so that our unconscious tends to produce peace and harmony rather than anxiety, aggravation, and dissatisfaction.

Some people are more likely to be at ease, some more likely to worry and hurry, some more likely to shout and slam doors, and some more likely to laugh. The idea of a karmic storehouse provides an explanation for why this is so. The idea that our past profoundly influences our present is central to Buddhist thought. Karma, which means "action" in its simplest definition, is a complex concept and is treated and understood variously throughout Buddhist and other Indian literature. In this context, it means the process by which our past actions, intentions, and emotional states influence what we experience and do in the present—and how, in the present, they influence our future.

The tendencies we have stored up in our alaya are known as "karmic seeds." When they manifest in the present moment they are known as "karmic fruit." The results of our present-moment intentions are known as "impressions." Our impressions produce seeds, which produce fruit, which produce impressions, and so on and so on. This process occurs in the store consciousness, though we could also say that the store consciousness *is* this process.

The idea of karma is generally understood to be something that carries over through many cycles of rebirth. Evidence suggests that Vasubandhu, the historical Buddha, and most Buddhists throughout history have believed that rebirth occurs, or at least that such a belief was helpful. These days, many Buddhists do not agree. Many teachings on karma don't refer to the idea of rebirth at all and make perfect sense without it. Vasubandhu's teachings on karma rarely allude to anything related to rebirth, and they make clear that we cannot know the contents of the storehouse. The power of our habits is evidence enough to me of the vastness of those stores of seeds, but whether they came from previous incarnations or not is outside of my knowledge. Whether rebirth occurs, and whether our karma is carried over from past lives and into future ones or not, has little bearing on the practice and value of this text's teachings. The "Thirty Verses" shows an understanding of what is here right now rather than in a previous life or a future one, not many eons ago, nor tomorrow. It shows a path with benefits that can be clearly seen in this very lifetime, in this very moment, and perhaps in some future incarnation.

We carry a lot of karmic seeds around, and they manifest in many ways. When I was working as a bike messenger in the nineties, I recall I was almost struck by a car on a snowy day in downtown Minneapolis. I felt a brief shock of fear as I dodged out of the way of the massive speeding machine, and then I felt rage. I furiously chased down the car, dodging traffic through icy streets as it sped away. When I caught up to it, I pounded on its frosty window, shouting. Eventually the driver, livid, drove off without ever opening the window. When I was exposed to the danger of the car, the seeds from the emotional reactions and survival strategies I developed as a young child; the seeds from all the time I spent with intense, often troubled and angry bike messengers; the seeds of cultural conditioning I internalized to transmute all bad feelings into aggression; and countless other seeds from countless generations manifested in the form of rage. It was very unpleasant to experience for me, and I acted in a way that was unkind, producing a very unpleasant experience for the driver that probably did not improve their attitude toward bicyclists. This way of conducting myself produced another impression, planted another seed of rage in my storehouse, that manifested many other times. However, the pain of that rage also touched other seeds: seeds from my past that made me want to be happy and at peace. I began to realize that yelling at dangerous drivers was not going to promote my welfare and the thing to do was take care of my reactivity, my consciousness. This was just as I was beginning Zen practice.

Recently another car almost hit me. I reflexively pulled over and dodged it. I noticed my racing heart and an angry thought, I noticed the leaves in the gutter, I saw the stricken face of the driver who'd realized what they'd done, I felt a flush of compassion for the two of us in this awkward situation, and I felt our deep connection to the billions of other people who are in danger, are afraid, who make mistakes, the whole thing. I felt at peace. The external situation was very similar to the first mishap, but there were different seeds in my storehouse this time, seeds of presence, seeds of peace, seeds of compassion, sown by Buddhist practice.

The store consciousness is a Yogacara innovation, but it has deep roots in Early Buddhist thought. Early Buddhism uses the term *bhavanga* to describe a similar aspect of consciousness, a ground of karmic activity below our awareness. In the Anguttara Nikaya, Buddha teaches, "Karma is intention, having intended, one does karma through body, speech, and mind." Karma produces intention, which produces actions of body, speech, and mind, which produce further karma.

Since there is suffering in our past, there is suffering in our present. Since there is kindness in our past, there is kindness in our present. But this is the main point: you have this moment of intention. This moment's intention—what you choose right now—is the key to whether you are moving toward more suffering or more kindness. Every single moment you have an opportunity to plant a beneficial karmic seed. In terms of what you can do with your life, your choice in this moment is what really matters. It is the endless point of return for Buddhist practice.

This does not mean that karma—previous intention—is the only thing that influences your life. In the *Sivaka Sutta*, Buddha makes it clear that in his view we experience many things that are not the result of karma. It is not karma that brings a tsunami to Indonesia, nor karma alone that gives you cancer. Just as Consciousness Only does not ultimately teach that consciousness is all that there is, but that it is best to concentrate on consciousness; likewise karma does not teach that our whole life is shaped by our past choices, but that, if we want to be well, we should concentrate on the choice we are making in this moment. Keeping the store consciousness in mind can help us remember that we have the capacity to plant healthy seeds that can bear fruit that is good for us, for our loved ones, and for everything.

There is a grave danger that the theory of karma will be used to blame the victims of horrible circumstances, by claiming that they are brought on by their karma. Karma should be used not to blame those whose suffer but to offer a message of empowerment. If you suffer from emotional and behavioral knots from traumatic experiences in the past, as I believe everyone to some degree does, the teaching of karma gives you the opportunity to practice freedom from these painful patterns.

In the second half of this verse, Vasubandhu begins to lay out some characteristics of the storehouse, as he will with the manas and the six senses in subsequent verses. The first characteristic is that what the storehouse holds and what it perceives as its surroundings are not something we can consciously know. What it holds is twofold: our body and our karma.

We say the store consciousness holds the body because somewhere deep in our unconscious mind there is a sense that our consciousness is attached to a physical form. In fact, underlying almost all human experience is a sense that we are located in a body. Oftentimes, our sense is that consciousness is located in the head. Neuroscientists, however, tell us that we can't actually locate consciousness in a physical place, and sometimes people dreaming, meditating, reacting to trauma, under the influence of drugs, or in various other circumstances experience consciousness as outside of the body. However, we generally have a conscious sense of being in our physical body.

We say that the storehouse's holding of the body is unknown because there are ways in which our consciousness relates to the body that are below or beyond our awareness. When we tie our shoes, it is very common that we have no awareness of what we're doing with our fingers and yet they execute an incredibly intricate dance to tie the knot; this is conditioning of the store consciousness manifesting with its sense of holding a body. It is possible, of course, to be mindful of tying our shoes, to bring awareness to the action, and this is a lovely practice. Our breath is also a bridge between our store consciousness taking up the body and our awareness of that body; it is a place where we can become aware of something that is usually unconscious. But although we can come closer to seeing the way our unconscious has a sense of having a body, ultimately there will always be something below thought: for example, the motion of the individual ventricles of the heart and the dilation of our eyes.

The storehouse also holds our karma. In each moment the store consciousness is processing karma; the impressions of our past are forming what the storehouse is anew. Just as a river can be called a river, but at no point is it ever identical to any other version of itself—the riffles of its surface, the water of its flowing, utterly unique in each moment—so we can say that there is a storehouse that is made of a flow of karma, but what that karma is, is always completely unique. This unique moment of karmic contents is what the storehouse holds, and we cannot directly see it. We can infer things about our karma, but we can't directly know it. In Buddhist practice we put some trust in our storehouse: if we plant beneficial seeds of kindness, generosity, mindful attention to our emotions, and wholehearted work, those seeds will bear fruit. This trust isn't so hard to find if we practice, as it is very easy to see the wellness appear in our lives when we do it.

We also can't know what the store consciousness perceives; it is perception operating below our conscious awareness. In the *Yogacarabhumi*, Vasubandhu's half-brother and the other great genius of Yogacara, Asanga, explains using the metaphor of a burning lamp. He compares the body to a wick, our karmic impressions to oil, and light to what the storehouse perceives. On one hand it is clear that a wick, oil, light, and the images the light illuminates are interdependent: none exists without the other. The key point here, though, is that what our unconscious perceives is limited and profoundly colored by our current state of body and karma. Picture a large cave lit by an oil lamp's flame; we see a tiny area of the floor and dim light disappearing into darkness in all directions. If the lamp burns high and steady, with clear fuel and a good wick, we may see the rough and lovely walls appear. If the flame is guttering and rough, we see a phantasmagoria of tortured shadows writhing on the walls. Before our perceptions even enter our conscious awareness as the six senses, there is this unconscious perception of the world, profoundly influenced by our karma and our body, that underlies what we believe is direct perception.

I recall once, as a young adolescent, I was living in London, far from my small hometown in Iowa. I was making a long walk home from the center of the city and took a new route. I became disoriented and began to feel a rising sense of panic, completely lost in a foreign city much larger than any I had known. As I walked, everything looked utterly unknown and frightening. My mind raced and my heart pounded. Suddenly in the middle of a large open square, I realized exactly where I was and that I had been there a dozen times before. I recognized everything as familiar. One step before, I had seen a dangerous, unknown city; in the next step, a well-known, comfortable spot near my home. The external world was the same, the processes in my storehouse were different. The karmic impressions of fear and disorientation and the racing heart and ragged breath all evaporated in the light of the karmic impressions of my memory of the place, and the nearness of a cup of milky tea.

It helps to know that what the storehouse perceives is unknown. It helps because it can remind us that what we are seeing—what we believe to be reality right now—is actually deeply and unknowably conditioned by our unconscious tendencies. This knowledge can help us let go when we are trying hard to control things, when we feel like we know exactly how everything should be. We don't even know how it really is; how can we know how it should be? When we are afraid, or anxious, or sad, we can remember that whatever is bringing us this feeling has only questionable reality. It helps to know that what the storehouse perceives is unknown because it may encourage us to do our meditation practice, to sow the seeds of wellness, so that the world our storehouse perceives doesn't have to be one full of fearful things, ugliness, and problems, but can instead be full of beauty and opportunities to do some small, helpful thing. Through upright sitting and the steady practice of compassionate action, the lamp of our store consciousness may come to cast a bright and steady light to guide the Way.

4

Aspects of the Buddhist Unconscious

It is always associated with sense-contact, attention,
sensation, perception, and volition,

Neither pleasant nor unpleasant.
It is unobstructed, and karmically neutral,

Like a river flowing. In enlightenment
it is overturned at its root. ‖ 4 ‖

Sense-contact, attention, sensation, perception, and volition—these are the five universal mental factors, which are always associated with the store consciousness. In order to understand the first line of this verse, we'll need to see their close relationship to the five aggregates, or *skandhas*, one of the oldest and most fundamental subjects of Buddhist teaching.

These aggregates—form, sensation, perception, formation, and consciousness—provide a way of describing experience. A key Early Buddhist practice was to see the five aggregates and realize that none of them were *I*, *me*, or *mine*. When one sees that nothing in our experience is truly ourself, the tendency to cling to things is shed—since there is no *I* that can cling—and we can be free of suffering.

The first of the aggregates, form, means the physical world: earth, water, air, and heat. The next, sensation, sometimes translated as "feeling-tone," is the very root-level and generally subconscious sense that we have in each of moment of "liking," "not liking," or "indifference." This is usually described as positive, negative, or neutral sensation. Perception, the third, is the ascribing of concepts to this basic sense data. When there is dark motion in our field of vision, that is form; when the mind conceptualizes it as a bird, that is perception; when it is large, there may be a positive sensation, as some minds are inclined to like large birds. Formation, the fourth aggregate, is the way that our karmic conditioning impels us to act. It is the intersection of our karma and our intention, and it often carries an emotional tone. I was raised by birders, so when perception recognizes a big bird and a positive sensation arises, a formation of excitement appears, and I desire to stop and look at it. Consciousness, the fifth aggregate, sometimes called "knowing," is awareness or cognizance. It has a distinct meaning in this five-aggregate schema. Generally in a case like this, my consciousness is awareness of the bird as a form in the visual field and as a perception: "An eagle!" But if I am mindful of the aggregates, I may also notice the formation, an excited emotion and impulse to point, the underlying sense of positive sensation, and form as it manifests in the way my body feels.

The five factors in this verse, which will reappear twice more in the "Thirty Verses," are a modified version of the five aggregates. The reworking of the five aggregates into the five universal factors was an innovation of the Abhidharma movement, in which Vasubandhu did his earlier studies and writing.

"Perception" and "sensation" from the five aggregates become two of the five universal mental factors, unchanged. "Form" is revamped into "sense-contact": the interaction between a sense organ, for example the ear, and a sense object, such as sound. By reframing this we seek to eliminate the problem of knowing whether what we are perceiving as form is real. For example I have tinnitus, a constant ringing in my ears. Also, right now, there are crickets singing outside the window. The sounds are extremely similar and sometimes indistinguishable. By calling the experience "sense-contact," and identifying a sound (singing and/or ringing) instead of a form (crickets?), I acknowledge that I don't ultimately know what is "out there"; I just know that there is some kind of sensory experience. "Form" implies that we experience a "thing" or object; sense-contact simply describes that there is a sensory occurrence.

The aggregate of consciousness is remade into "attention" in this system. In Early Buddhist texts the term *consciousness* usually means "awareness," but sometimes it refers to that which enters into the womb when a person embarks on a new rebirth. By using the term *attention* the Abidharma and this text give us one definition and one aspect of experience we can attend to: awareness, or more precisely, where our awareness is directed.

Formation, or volitional tendency, is remade here into "volition." In momentary terms we can notice that we have an impulse or choice to do something, a volition. We can't, however, directly experience the past conditions that create that volition; as we saw in verse 3, what the storehouse holds (its karma) can't be known. The aggregate called "formation" includes both of these aspects—volition and conditioning—but Vasubandhu, using the Abidharma approach, divides

How the Elements of the Three Ways of Categorizing Experience Correspond		
Five Aggregates	**Five Universal Mental Factors**	**Six Conciousnesses; the All**
Form	Sense Contact	sight, sound, smell, taste, touch
Consciousness	Attention	thought
Sensation	Sensation	
Perception	Perception	
Formation	Volition	

and isolates them. He gives us "volition" to investigate in the moment as one of the five universal mental factors, and then he deals extensively with the issue of conditioning throughout this text, using the metaphor of karmic seeds. Thus these two aspects of the aggregate called "formation" are separated.

To recap: Sense-contact is a nonconceptualized moment of sensory experience. Attention is the mind being aware of some particular aspect of the moment. Sensation is a very basic, generally subconscious sense of positivity, negativity, or neutrality. Perception is the ascribing of conceptual labels to things. Volition is the impulse or inclination to act, generally characterized by an emotion. Being aware of these universal factors occurring through mindfulness meditation allows us to see that they are not *I*, *me*, or *mine*—they are just things that are happening—and thus helps us let go of our ego-centered tendency to cling to things. We will investigate meditation practice with the five universal factors in a few chapters.

The second line of this verse refers to a kind of neutrality that characterizes the store consciousness. It doesn't have a positive or negative sensation, it isn't obstructed by afflictive emotion or delusion, and it does not itself create or record karma. This is a little confusing as the karmic processes in the store consciousness produce sensations, affliction, and further karma, which we experience as a sense of self and the imagery of sense objects. The storehouse is not the seeds, though neither is it separate from them. The point is that the storehouse itself is neutral; it is simply a space where karmic processes occur. It can be full of rotting corn or fresh organic greens, but once those are gone, it is just a neutral space ready for the next contents. Even when you find yourself overwhelmed by fear, grief, anger, or confusion, you still have the chance to plant a seed of compassionate awareness and find a moment of peace. Sometimes the power of our conditioning—that thicket of thorns—is so dense that our intention to be present and kind seems like a puff of cotton in the wind, but that small effort may allow that seed to land and someday grow into the broad shade of a cottonwood tree, where weary travelers find rest. Because of the neutrality of the store consciousness there is room for infinite change and growth. Every moment is your opportunity.

The store consciousness is like a river flowing. We can describe it as a solid thing for practical purposes, but it is only a process of change. It is a momentary phenomenon that is nominally described to help us be well. It is not lasting, separate, or permanent. The earliest Yogacara text, the *Samdhinirmocana Sutra*, states:

The storehouse consciousness is very profound
    and subtle;

All its seeds are like a torrential flow.
I do not explain it to the ignorant,
For fear they will cling to it and consider it a self.

As Heraclitus perfectly put it, "You cannot step in the same river twice."

A river is powerful and ineluctable. Forces infinitely old come together to make the river what it is in this moment. Sometimes heat-beaten wayfarers may come to take cool water on the banks along with all the wild things, at other times the waters rise in great flood and tear away trees and bridges, sweeping away those who come too close. Sometimes our conditioning allows us to be a cool place for others to find respite, and other times we cause harm. The river itself is beyond our control, but by attending to our minds we can become aware of how it swells, how it banks, and how it slowly flows. We don't really see the river, the store consciousness, but we can see how the force of our conditioning is creating this moment of emotion and in this way be a little less likely to be swept away by it. We can take care of what's right before us, our own on-flowing heart.

A basic teaching of Buddhism tells us that we can let go of karma and find complete rest: nirvana. This third line says that in nirvana, the entire process of karma that occurs in the storehouse is overturned; there is a revolution at the root of consciousness, sometimes called a transformation at the base.

I have not attained nirvana. I'm still affected by karma, I see my past habits emerge in my life, and I suffer and cause harm. However it's very common in Consciousness Only literature to speak of a revolution at the root or consciousness that makes the store consciousness into great mirror wisdom that perfectly reflects without obscuration or coloration—a vast mind untainted by afflictive emotions, delusion, or conditioning. Though I'm still bound to this river of karma, I have confidence based in experience that you can begin to sense this mirror through practice. You can allow for the complete transformation of consciousness into something purely available to and manifesting what is, whose every action is made from the perspective of universal connection, infinite compassion.

5

Mind Makes Self and Other

Dependent on the store consciousness
and taking it as its object,

Manas, the consciousness of a self, arises,
which consists of thinking. ‖ 5 ‖

The manas, or consciousness of a self, is (along with the store consciousness) a defining Yogacara innovation. The idea that we have a sense of being *I*, that we think there are things that are *me* and *mine*, is central to many forms of Buddhist thought, but the idea that there is an aspect of consciousness that creates this sense of self is distinctly Yogacarin. The manas consciousness, depending on the karma of the store consciousness, believes part of experience to be self, *I*, and in so doing it causes the other aspects of experience to appear to be *other*.

An important part of the practice laid out in Early Buddhist sutras is seeing that the five aggregates— form, sensation, perception, mental formations, and consciousness—are not-self. That is to say, realizing that bodily sensations, and the body itself, is not *I*, *me*, or *mine*; impulses to act are not *I, me*, or *mine*; being aware is not *I, me*, or *mine*. We see this through nonjudgmentally observing things arise and go away, seeing that all phenomena, including those that we'd normally categorize as being "ourselves," are just fleeting things that are happening. As this realization deepens, our tendency to get stuck on our desires fades. For example, instead of thinking, "I need my son to clean this room," we can be aware that there is tension in the body and mind, along with images of clothing scattered on the floor in our field of vision, and impulses to speak in a loud and angry voice. This allows us to take care of the suffering that is right in front of us (in what is conventionally thought to be our own body and mind) and then act truly on behalf of our child, speaking kindly, to help him have a clean space and healthful habits, rather than trying to control him in order to alleviate our own suffering, the pain of our own anger and judgment.

In an Early Buddhist sutra, written long before the idea of manas was developed, we see a seed of its development. An old and ill monk is visited by some younger monks. They ask him whether he has seen, through his practice, that the five aggregates are not-self, to which he answers in the affirmative, but he goes on to say that he still experiences "the residual conceit, 'I am.'" This old monk is in essence saying that he still experiences manas.

He's talking about his own direct experience, not parroting teachings or trying to show off his attainments. He is attached to his self and his life, albeit in a very soft and wise way, and he shows these young monks, as he nears death, not a magical message of liberation, nor a religiously correct view, but merely what he knows from his own deep practice of looking at life coming and going. In the *Yogacarabhumi*, one of the most comprehensive Yogacara texts, whose authorship is not known, manas is defined using this same language: "Manas . . . is conceiving, I-making, the conceit 'I am.'" The honesty and depth of practice of one old monk was carried through hundreds of years to the *Yogacarabhumi* and right into this text and our minds, right now.

This manas creates the sense that our hand is our own, that our thoughts are our own, that we are looking out at a world from inside our bodies. It is central to our sense of separation and alienation, but it's also a fundamental and useful aspect of a healthy human consciousness. Psychologists tell us babies develop a sense of self, manas, in their first year. Before their egos develop, they cry when they are tired, or hungry, or grumpy until someone takes care of their needs. Over the years we need to develop a sense of self-regulation and autonomy so that when things are difficult we don't have to be overwhelmed, and so we can allow who we are as unique aspects of the universe to flower for our own well-being and for everyone. We need to make our own lunches, clean our own rooms, take care of our personal boundaries, and make our own particular offerings—whatever they may be. The first half of the "Thirty Verses" presents a model for developing a healthy ego by working with consciousness, one that is not overcome by afflictive emotion, that softens and doesn't need to hold on so tightly. The second half gives a means to see through and let go of the sense of self.

Many people in many traditions have described experiences of life without any sense of being a self separate from other things. The language of these descriptions tends in this way: boundless, infinite, compassionate, joyful, emptiness, intimate, blissful. One young man came to me for a practice meeting a few months after he'd woken from a coma. As he came back to the world his consciousness was not producing a sense of separateness. He'd felt deep peace and unity with everything, and major problems he'd had with his family were completely gone. But as the effects of the coma faded, the boundless appreciation and connection faded, and he wanted to do Zen practice to get it back. It was an amazing story, and I was pained to follow the best way I know and to tell him he shouldn't try to get that back, that pursuing that sense would only feed the karma of desire that makes the manas afflicted. I encouraged him to practice just to be in life right now as it is, for this is the way to plant the seeds in the storehouse that grow to a sense of boundless intimacy.

This verse says manas "consists of thinking," and indeed the word *manas* is a common Sanskrit word that means "thinking." Yogacarins use this word in a particular and technical way. In this case *thinking* does not just mean having word-based thoughts moving through the mind. As we will see in a couple of verses, the manas is almost always functioning, even when there are not what we'd usually call "thoughts." This verse provides a particular, technical definition of thinking: *I*-making, or having the sense of being a self.

Here Vasubandhu merely begins a description of manas as a basic aspect of consciousness. Although it is intimately associated with how it comes to be that people suffer and cause harm, and although Vasubandhu will describe at the end of these verses that its cessation is vast, blissful, compassionate liberation, we are not instructed here to reject it. The path laid forth here is to know it, be intimate with it, see it manifesting here in this moment. The way to practice with manas is to be aware, to be attentive, to take care of it.

6

Stuck on the Self

It is always associated with four afflictions, self-view,
self-delusion, self-pride, and self-love,

And is obstructed but karmically neutral.
Along with these four, ‖ 6 ‖

Manas, the consciousness that creates a self, is intimately related to our tendency to be dissatisfied, to
suffer. It gives rise to a focus on the self that results in
confusion about the nature of what's happening in the
moment—creating tendencies known as "afflictions"
because they cause us to suffer.

In his first discourse Buddha teaches what he
describes as the Noble Eightfold Path: right view, right
intention, right speech, right action, right livelihood,
right effort, right mindfulness, and right concentration. Life, he says, is characterized by *dukkha*, dissatisfaction and suffering, caused by wanting things to be
other than they are; the Eightfold Path offers a practical
model for promoting well-being, a model of healing. In
later teachings, dukkha is described in more detail as
kleshas, afflictions.

The most well-known kleshas are desire, aversion, and delusion: things that arise in consciousness and are painful, or create dissatisfaction. Further along in the "Thirty Verses" we will see some more extensive lists of afflictions, and here in this verse we encounter four: self-view, self-delusion, self-pride, and self-love.

The word *klesha* is sometimes translated as "defilement," but "affliction" is a much more accurate and helpful translation of this term. In Sanskrit, *klesha* generally carries the meaning of affliction or illness, not defilement or a lack of purity. Importantly, by describing what arises in mind and causes harm as an affliction, an illness, we are more easily moved toward compassion, toward a nonjudgmental impulse to heal. The language of "defilement" and "purity" can easily give rise to shame and pride. When we see afflictions, on the other hand, we have an opportunity to be present to the suffering and open our hearts to the possibility of wellness.

Vasubandhu tells us that when manas is functioning, which is during most of human experience, these afflictions arise: self-view, self-delusion, self-pride, and self-love. Self-view is having the viewpoint, or sense, that there is a self. Self-delusion is being confused about what the self is. Self-pride is placing undue importance on oneself in relation to other things. And self-love is clinging to the self's interest in a way that causes suffering.

A quick reading of these can give pause, for it seems that a few of these are actually fundamental aspects of a healthy, functioning person. Without self-view how would one know to leave an abusive relationship? This is one of the reasons that we are not instructed by Vasubandhu to somehow immediately amputate the manas. There are certainly Buddhist teachings, and many other mystic teachings, that encourage us to urgently and permanently drop away the self, but Vasubandhu in this first half of the "Thirty Verses" is deeply attuned to the psychological precision of the Early Buddhist model of practice. The Buddha's Eight-fold Path does include letting the sense of self go in deep states of concentration, but it also includes being and seeing the self as it is right now through ethical activity and mindfulness.

Self-view is helpful if a car is coming our way at high speed as we cross a street; it is a natural aspect of human consciousness designed for self-protection. Unfortunately it clouds our view so we don't realize our total and profound connection to everything else, our capacity for self-preservation becomes obsessive, and we lose the vast spacious capacity of mind.

Self-delusion is the profundity of our confusion about who we are, which manifests in the form of certainty. Who are you? What are you? Who am I? These should instead be viewed as koans: practice questions whose value never dies, because if we dive into the question we see that there is no ultimate answer. Every idea we have about ourselves is delusion, and yet we often conduct ourselves as if our ideas are ironclad facts.

Self-pride is seeing ourselves in relation to everything else inaccurately—seeing ourselves as much more important than we are in the grand scheme of things. The term is a little confusing as it has two aspects; our view of ourself might be excessively positive or negative. For instance, if I'm thinking about how I know more than the fellow next to me about Yogacara, the affliction of self-pride is manifesting, cutting me off from my experience, my fellow, and the teaching. And if I'm thinking about how I am awful at gardening, or am a terrible mother, that too is self-pride; for I have cut myself off from what is happening through preconceptions about my relation to plants or children. I am not seeing my real relationship. Self-pride is the tendency to see ourselves as the bump on the universe.

Self-love is not about a healthy sense of self-esteem. Self-love is about clinging: clinging to what we want, clinging to life, and also pushing away what we don't like. Often, afflicted by self-love, we eat just because we want to get some pleasure for ourselves, but it is possible to eat food not because you want it or it's your favorite kind, but because you realize you have the capacity to be of service to others and you can't do it without food. During formal meals on Zen retreats we chant, "we regard this food as medicine to sustain our life . . . for the sake of enlightenment we now receive this food." It is possible and quite wonderful to eat without self-love, to eat with love for everything.

All of these appear in gross and subtle forms. Sometimes when I am angry and self-pride becomes very intense, I begin to feel very sure that I am right. I get tense and my mind churns over and over, imagining arguments I'll never have. However, according to these verses and my experience, these four afflictions arise in subtle forms even when the mind is very, very quiet. Even in the fading light of the last sitting of a beautiful day devoted to meditation practice, this residual conceit "I am" is often there, quietly making a subtle sense of dissatisfaction. How soon will the bell ring? I hope the bell never rings!

Vasubandhu says this manas is "obstructed, but karmically neutral." Even though it always arises with these four afflictions, and is thus obstructed, it, like the store consciousness, is not inherently negative. The manas is a space where these obscurations occur, but it can be transformed into clarity. In many Yogacara teachings, as the seeds of wellness are cultivated in the storehouse through practice, the storehouse is transformed into the great mirror wisdom, and the manas is transformed into the wisdom of equality. Rather than placing the self at the center of everything and constantly trying to control things to suit the self, the transformed manas appears merely as a way of seeing the equality and value of everything that appears, leaving behind judgments and manifesting total compassion for everything in every moment.

7

Seeing Through *I*, *Me*, and *Mine*

From where it is born come sense-contact, attention, sensation, perception, and volition.

It is not found in enlightenment, the meditation of cessation, or the supramundane path. ‖ 7 ‖

Manas is born in each moment, because karma and other conditions arise in a way that supports its birth. In this verse these conditions are called "from where it is born." *Here* is the place; the fact that you and I have a sense of being a self is the result of infinite conditions arising in this moment. The evolution of fur-bearing mammals, the way your parents taught you your name through countless repetitions, the effectiveness with which our categorizing minds have perpetuated the human species, the billboards that remind you that you should keep wanting things you don't have, the pleasure you took from drinking tea this morning, the anger you felt when your mother criticized your housekeeping, the breath that is passing through your body right now—these are the ground for the place, this moment, where manas is born. The energy that has gone into creating a sense of self is vast beyond measure. Although our sense of a self is a basic aspect of why we suffer and cause harm, it is also just one of the infinite manifestations of the way things are. Let's not make it an enemy. We can practice in a way that is kind to manas, that allows a transformation, that plants seeds of karma that can grow into a mind that is free of this sense of alienation from the moment, that clearly sees and is available to whatever appears.

Depending on conditions "where it is born," manas arises with the five universal mental factors: sense-contact, attention, sensation, perception, and volition. Having introduced these in chapter 4, I will not discuss them here, though I will address them extensively as an object of meditation in chapter 10. Instead, let's focus on the main theme of this verse: the conditions in which manas is not found.

As we will see toward the end of the "Thirty Verses," Vasubandhu and Yogacara in general place the split between subject and object, self and other, at the very center of the problem of human suffering. Since the afflicted manas creates this split, by definition, its cessation is key. The conditions in which Vasubandhu says the afflicted manas is not found are enlightenment, the meditation of cessation, and the supramundane (bodhisattva) path.

By including all three of these, Vasubandhu, as is

often the case, makes a way for divergent ideas to live happily under one roof. Many other texts in many other Buddhist traditions over the years have made fierce doctrinal arguments, claiming their side was right. Vasubandhu devotes his vast knowledge of Buddhist thought and his deep practice, over and over again, to demonstrating how all these views can work together.

The meditation of cessation is a state of meditation that many yogis and Buddhists described, where their consciousness appeared to completely stop functioning. A monk would sit, enter the meditation of cessation, and hours later come back to the realm of form having had no experience, and no sense of a self having had an experience. That the manas was not functioning seemed clear, but when people came back from this meditation they were still carrying their old karma around; they had all their old memories, and they often saw the same emotional habits arise. This is why we say the afflicted manas isn't found in the meditation of cessation, but the store consciousness still functions in it. Deep meditative states, called *right concentration* in the Eightfold Path, are a valuable aspect of the path to liberation. However deep meditative states are not the ultimate aspiration of Buddhist practice; the root aspiration is the alleviation of suffering.

Early Buddhists, and Theravadans today, revere arhats who have attained nirvana, the cessation of suffering. Mahayana Buddhists, on the other hand, view bodhisattvas who have devoted their lives to alleviating suffering in others as the great exemplars of the path. In this verse Vasubandhu tells us that manas is not found in enlightenment, the state of being one who has attained nirvana, nor in the supramundane path, a common Indian term for the state of being a bodhisattva. Many texts in the respective traditions agree with this assertion: the arhat sees that he or she can't locate his or her self in anything, the bodhisattva realizes that nothing at all has its own selfhood, including his or her self. Vasubandhu is finding common ground. Early Buddhists describe nirvana as a state where there is no suffering, no desire, no aversion, no delusion. When there is no manas there is the profound peace that comes from not wanting things to be other than they are. Mahayana texts describe the bodhisattva manifesting infinite compassionate activity. When there is no manas, the activity of human form is always directed to taking care of everything that appears in the moment in the kindest possible way. The "Thirty Verses" declares that the best way to realize both of these ideals is to do both the Early Buddhist practices of observing the emotional tendencies of mind and the Mahayana practice of radically nondual meditation. In a few chapters we'll begin to dig into the former, and in the second half of the book we'll delve deeper into the Mahayana ocean of interdependence, emptiness, and thusness.

8
The All

That is the second transformation,
the third is the perception of the six senses,

Which are beneficial, harmful, or neither. || 8 ||

In the second verse of this text, Vasubandhu told us there were three aspects of the transformation of consciousness: the ripening of karma, the consciousness of a self, and the imagery of sense objects. Having described the first two, he will now move on to the third, which he calls here "the perception of the six senses," the six senses being sight, sound, smell, taste, touch, and mind.

This is the aspect of consciousness of which we are generally aware. This is what we call "experience." Right now, as I write, there is the sound of cicadas, the roar of a distant plane, a complex array of visual images, thoughts manifesting through the motion of fingers as words on a page, a sense of connection with you. This moment of experience is the ground for our opportunity to practice. The Buddha way is to alleviate suffering, and it is in, or through, this All—these six senses—that we do it.

This verse says the perception of the six senses is beneficial, harmful, or neither. This means that we can choose to act in a way that manifests the intention to alleviate suffering—or not. The approach the "Thirty Verses" presents for the alleviating of suffering is remarkable in that it deals almost exclusively with one thing: awareness of whether what is occurring as a manifestation of our mental tendencies in this moment is beneficial or afflictive; awareness of how we feel.

The basis of meditation practice in Early Buddhism is mindfulness of body. In Zen we practice *just sitting*, or *posture and breath*. Vipassana teachers call their students back again and again to awareness of the breath, the body, or sound as objects of concentration. Vasubandhu does not spend much time on this subject here, but all the teachings he will provide on seeing our mental tendencies are rooted in the "perception of the six senses." We can only know these mental tendencies through what is arising in the body (touch), sound, sight, smell, taste, and mind. In particular mindfulness of the body is a powerful basis for developing the concentration necessary to see what is arising emotionally and also a very effective way of being intimate with it. If we practice mindfulness of body, we will begin to see how ragged breath comes with anger and anxiety, slumping posture comes with sadness, deep breaths and a strong upright body come with tranquility and joy.

Deepening into our awareness of the six senses in

general is a wonderful means to draw ourselves to the present and let go of the tendency to direct all of our attention into imagining the future, rehashing the past, or judging the present. Recently I stood by the shore of the urban lake by our Zen center gazing at the light of a setting sun playing across the water and the sky. Many people of many races and languages were running, biking, and strolling by, but all stopped and simply gave their attention to the effulgence all around. We stopped and drank deeply of the radiance and, in so doing, there came to be some peace. I think I was probably not the only one in that moment who noticed the stillness in my heart.

The next six verses will focus on mindfulness of our mental states as the principal means to overcome the barrier of afflictive emotion.

In the *Abhidharmakosa*, Vasubandhu states, "There is no other way of pacifying the afflictions than through the discernment of dharmas, the sole purpose for which Abhidharma was taught."

Remember, Abhidharmists developed a system for categorizing dharmas, different types of phenomena or moments of experience. They include things like eye, ear, seeing consciousness, sense-contact, aspiration, desire, faith, anger, distraction, remorse, volition, birth/arising, continuity/decay, time, and thusness. The practice was to memorize the list of dharmas and then be mindful of and discerning of these dharmas, as they appear in the moment. In the "Thirty Verses," Vasubandhu presents a partial list of these dharmas, divided into two types. The first is the five universal mental factors that we have encountered a few times already, and the second is emotional/volitional tendencies, or formations: specific, beneficial, afflictive, and indeterminate. By listing these dharmas, he's telling us that two forms of practice are most beneficial: mindfulness of the universal factors and mindfulness of our current emotional state. These are the methods Vasubandhu recommends for overcoming afflictive emotion.

How do you deal with afflictive emotion? People have many ways. Generally we are not even aware that we are experiencing affliction. For example, rather than knowing that they are angry, some people are likely to think (and erroneously believe) that their ex-wives are capricious and cruel. Rather than knowing that I am frustrated, I sometimes think (or am entranced by thoughts about the idea that) people in Minnesota don't know how to drive in snow. It is a deep and powerful aspect of human karmic tendency to try and externalize emotion and focus on judging and trying to control apparently external objects so that we may feel well. Vasubandhu is telling us that purchasing a new smartphone, trying to manipulate our family members, swearing at people in other cars, and running over the same old ground of our dreams of escape from our very own lives are all pretty ineffective at promoting wellness. In "The Song of the Grass-Roof Hermitage," Shitou teaches, "Turn around the light to shine within." If we really want to be well, let's learn to see and take care of our mental states. We can cultivate ones that are beneficial and let go of ones that are harmful. Thus we plant the seeds for more beneficial mind-states and fewer harmful ones. We will see that we don't need to be aggressive and controlling about this cultivating and letting go; the method centers on simply being aware and attentive to who we are in this moment, here and now.

9

Mindfulness of Phenomena

It is associated with three kinds of mental factors: universal, specific, and beneficial,

As well as the afflictions and secondary afflictions, and the three sensations. || 9 ||

In this verse Vasubandhu begins to subdivide the six senses into a variety of categories, so that we may more effectively use them as objects of meditation and mindfulness. This categorization is rooted in Early Buddhist teachings and drawn directly from the Abhidharma. The Abhidharma is quite complex so this chapter will be as well, but over the next few chapters we'll be able to put this information to good use for cultivating joy, compassion, and equanimity.

All the material in the next few chapters will relate to practicing right effort and right mindfulness from the Eightfold Path. Right effort in simplest terms is making an endeavor such that what occurs in mind is conducive to wellness rather than harm. Right mindfulness is to be aware in the moment of specific things in a way that is conducive to wellness.

In most cases when right effort comes up in Early Buddhist texts, it is explained with a four-part formula that I'll paraphrase here: making effort so that harmful states do not arise, harmful states that have arisen cease, beneficial states arise, and beneficial states that are present continue. We can see that the last phrase in the last chapter's verse is pointing toward right effort—the six senses can be beneficial, harmful, or neither. The point is that right here, this moment of experiencing the six senses, is where we can apply right effort: doing laundry, walking the dog, or talking to our children.

In Zen practice, where I've done most of my training, right effort, as an attempt to control the mind, is de-emphasized. We tend to put more emphasis on just being aware of what's here without trying to judge or control, which is a subtle and very powerful expression of right effort. However there is room for right effort, in its most assertive sense, in anyone's practice. Sometimes when you see yourself beginning to dive into one of those stories you've told yourself a thousand times—"no one understands me," "I can't get anything right," "I'm always surrounded by fools . . ."—whatever that story is, sometimes it's possible to just say, "This story is not helping anyone," let it go, and move on. Sometimes we are in a position where we can just make a choice without being harsh or cruel to ourselves and change our minds for the better. However, sometimes this is not possible or advised. If the karmic energy of a mind-state is too strong, we may not be able to change it through will. Often as well, it's more helpful to just observe what the mind is doing with an open, kind curiosity and let it quiet down on its own. This state of openness is actually a very beneficial mind-state. Manifesting awareness of mind without trying to control it is an excellent way to practice right effort, and it is also known as right mindfulness.

Mindfulness basically means being aware of something. Right mindfulness is being aware, kindly and dispassionately, of specific things in a way that is conducive to well-being. The four foundations of mindfulness, as delineated in the eponymous sutra, are mindfulness of body, sensation, mind, and dharmas. Vasubandhu recommends that we focus our mindfulness practice on objects that are not exactly the same as, but are deeply connected to, the categories laid forth in that sutra: the universal, specific, and beneficial factors, afflictions and secondary afflictions, and the three sensations.

We investigated the universal mental factors—sense-contact, attention, sensation, perception, and volition—in chapter 4. The specific factors are somewhat of an outlier here and I will address them in the next chapter. The "three sensations" refers to the third universal factor, the very basic sense of positive, negative, or neutral that underlies our experience. In verse 4 Vasubandhu says the alaya is "neither pleasant nor unpleasant," which means the sensation there is neutral. Here he makes explicit that the sensation in the six senses, our direct experience, can have all three aspects.

Beneficial and afflictive states are karmic formations: emotional and volitional tendencies, the intersection of karma and intention; for example, anger, equanimity, envy, energy, or tranquility. These beneficial factors, afflictions, and secondary afflictions are both where we can see how the karma in the store consciousness is manifesting and where we can make effort to plant seeds of wellness in the storehouse. Vasubandhu's teaching here is that if we want to promote wellness it is absolutely key to focus on and attend to our emotional and volitional state. How do you feel right now? Just to see and be aware of what is manifesting is already a seed that can grow amazing and nourishing fruit.

These teachings may seem extremely complex, but at root they point in one direction, to the idea that we can transform the tendencies of mind so that consciousness manifests states of wellness rather than affliction, so that we may be at peace rather than suffering, so that we may be free of the painful states that limit our capacity to serve others.

10

Five Aggregates,
Five Universal Factors

The universal factors are sense-contact,
attention, sensation, perception, and volition.

The specific are aspiration, resolve, memory,
concentration, and intellection. || 10 ||

This verse deals with two types of mental phenomenon: the five universal mental factors we've addressed earlier in the book and the specific mental factors.

These specific factors are so named because, unlike the universals, they only arise in certain circumstances. They pose some difficulties for understanding; over the last fifteen hundred years, commentators have disagreed as to whether the specific mental factors are beneficial or not. Each of the items in this list of specific factors is a translation of a Sanskrit word that in Early Buddhist texts is considered beneficial. In fact three of them are included in a list called "the thirty-seven aids to enlightenment": *chanda*, aspiration; *smrti*, mindfulness/memory; and *samadhi*, concentration. The disagreement is whether these five specific factors are actually beneficial or are neutral factors that have the same names as things considered beneficial in other contexts, terms whose meaning evolved substantially during the development of the Abhidharma system. Both sides are persuasive, so I am choosing not to take sides. I'd like instead to focus in this chapter on the powerful and time-honored practice of working with the five universal mental factors.

Vasubandhu does not himself give us instructions for how to practice with the universal mental factors; he was writing in a context in which anyone reading this text would be expected to know what the practice associated with them was. By including them here he holds practicing with them up as fundamental to the way of liberation. Since these five mental factors are basically a renaming and reconceptualizing of the five aggregates, I will base these practice instructions on Pali Canon texts about working with the aggregates. The two main themes of these teachings is to observe the five arising, existing, and passing away, and to realize that they are not *I*, *me*, or *mine*.

To practice with the five—sense-contact, attention, sensation, perception, and volition—we must first know and remember them. Sense-contact is a moment of sense data: a sound, a color, a bodily feeling. Attention is the directionality of mind, where awareness is aimed.

Sensation is a very base-level sense that something is pleasant, unpleasant, or neutral. Perception is the ascribing of basic concepts, often names, to sense data. Volition is the impulse or inclination to do something. Here's an example: you feel an itch and scratch yourself. If you are practicing mindfulness of the five universal factors, you notice the following: sense-contact, a sensory experience in the body with no concepts or value attached to it; attention directing awareness to the sensory experience; sensation arising that deems the feeling unpleasant; perception calling it "itch"; and volition arising, seeking to scratch.

We practice mindfulness of the five universals/ aggregates by seeing what is arising in the moment and labeling it according to these categories. If we do this, something will happen that is rather interesting. Rather than thinking, "I have an itch, I want to scratch it," we see that there is sense-contact, attention, sensation, perception, and volition happening, in this very particular way, right now. We see a process happening that forms a sense of *I*, of *itch*, of *want*, of *unpleasant*. If we practice this in seated meditation and stay still for a little while, it is likely that we will also see all these things pass away. Watching these aggregates arise and fade and allowing that to soften our sense of *I* is a profoundly powerful means to weaken the karma that drives us to constantly be dissatisfied, that makes a brief moment of sense contact into something we must judge and control. Rather than acting on unconscious impulses we can be aware of the process of their coming and going.

It's important to note that the labeling of the aggregates should have a softness to it. The naming is there to help us actually be intimate with the experience. The point isn't to sit and think about sense-contact but to actually see the changing evening light moving across the wall without naming or judging, to deeply know the motion of the breathing belly, to truly feel the keys of this keyboard as I type. The point is to deeply experience the arising of a volition, an impulse to act, at the very moment of its arrival and to know it, to sense its texture, its shape. When we are about to berate a small child we have just stopped from running into the street, we can be aware of the racing heart, the clenched hand, the concepts proliferating about the child's foolishness, the intense unpleasant sensation of fear and loss of control, the impulse to shout—and we can take a moment to let this arise and pass, see that it is not "I," but an occurrence, deeply colored by the process of karma, in consciousness. We can see that the child is safe now; we don't need to unconsciously teach this child that to alleviate your own fear you should try and control other people. We can say something kind, and firm, and helpful, and we can be honest about how it feels to see the child in danger. We can foster connection and safety and plant seeds of kind speech and compassion for ourselves and for the world.

Recall that these five universals are associated with the store consciousness, manas, and the six senses. In verse 4, Vasubandhu teaches that even in the bodhisattva state—the supramundane path, where there is no afflicted manas—these five still appear in the store consciousness. I'll use a Zen koan to illustrate how these five mental factors appear, even when there is no sense of *I*, of subject and object.

> Yunyan asked Daowu, "How does the bodhisattva of compassion use all those hands and eyes?" Daowu answered, "It is like someone reaching behind her head for a pillow in the night."

Kuan Yin, the bodhisattva of compassion, is usually depicted with countless arms outstretched to help all the suffering of the world, and in each hand is an eye, to see and be present to that suffering. The bodhisattva has left behind almost every trace of her own karma through years of practice, but still some traces remain, allowing her to stay in the world and not forget how it is to suffer, not forget how close her life is to everyone else's. All over East Asia people call on the image, idea, and aid of Kuan Yin when they face illness, death, divorce, and despair. Many, too, follow her inspiration to a life of love and service. And yet, although she deeply hears countless cries and extends her loving arms of aid ceaselessly in all directions, she is as relaxed as someone reaching for a pillow in the night.

To reach for a pillow the five universal factors must still manifest. There is sense-contact, the sensory experience of the bed; attention, a directionality of mind toward bodily sensation; the sensation of unpleasantness, of suffering; the perception far below the level of thought that this can be alleviated; the volition to reach out and move the pillow to a nice comfy spot. This describes a profoundly easeful, unselfconscious, calm motion toward making things better. The reason Kuan Yin can have the energy to use a thousand hands and eyes to help and intimately hear people in their smallest and most terrible sufferings is that each gesture of each hand, each experience of seeing suffering, is unbounded by the self-centeredness, need, and focus on results that is made by manas. By seeing and being intimate with the five universal mental factors with mindfulness, we can see that they are not *I*, *me*, or *mine*; we plant the karmic seeds that lead toward the softening and dissolution of the afflicted manas. We water the seeds of opening our eyes and reaching out to help with no need to succeed or gain anything.

11

Cultivating Seeds of Goodness

The beneficial factors are faith, conscience, humility,
lack of desire, aversion, and delusion,

Energy, tranquility, carefulness,
equanimity, and nonviolence. || 11 ||

There are many ways to cultivate the seeds of goodness.

If we cultivate these seeds with our own mind and actions, their benefits go on forever. If nonviolence arises in the mind, an action will arise that is kind, the seeds of kindness will be planted in the storehouse, and we create the conditions for beneficial seeds in the storehouse of others.

Although a tiny moment of beneficial mind and action may seem insignificant in the vast ocean of time and space, it is, in fact, all we have to offer. It is the best we can do. No matter who you are, right now you have an opportunity to contribute to the universe something transformative and precious: your own beneficial intention. If you are making lunch and you do it with energy, tranquility, carefulness, and equanimity, you condition your mind to take care of the basics of life in this active, calm way. If you are enraged at the president of the United States for using your tax money to kill people and you take a moment to cultivate the faith that there is a way to alleviate suffering and to take care of the turmoil in your mind through nonviolence, you plant the seeds of commitment to alleviate suffering through kind action in your mind, and you may well find a way to go out and inch our world just a little bit further from its long cycle of violence and war. If you are completely depressed and lost in despair, and you cultivate faith in the possibility of well-being and accepting who you are with equanimity, you plant the seeds of hope through radical acceptance. You plant the seeds that can grow into a beautiful capacity to meet life, however and whoever it is, in each moment with energy, tranquility, lack of desire, nonviolence, and faith that this tiny moment of intention is your opportunity to contribute to the possibility of universal well-being.

I am talking about right effort: putting energy into cultivating beneficial mental states. We cannot climb into the store consciousness with a wrench and change the way it operates so that we are always happy and always do the most kind and helpful thing. The contents of storehouse are unconscious, beyond our knowing. What we can see are the six senses, and what Vasubandhu is suggesting we focus on—if we want to promote wellness—is the aspect of mind (the sixth sense) that is emotional and volitional. If we cultivate beneficial mind-states, principally through being mindfully aware of them as they arise but also by thinking and talking about them, encouraging each other to cultivate them, we can transform the storehouse. Consciousness tends to create the same kinds of things it's seen before. Seeds of peace grow peace, which plants seeds of peace.

This verse lays out eleven of the fifty-five dharmas or mental factors listed in the "Thirty Verses"; these fifty-five are part of an Abhidharma list of one hundred dharmas. Vasubandhu leaves out forty-five and includes only those that are either tied to very basic meditation practice (the universal factors) or have to do with our emotional and volitional impulses (the specific, beneficial, and afflictive factors). These verses provide a way of describing moment-to-moment experience in terms of the things most fundamental to our ability to liberate ourselves from emotional conditioning.

These big lists are a subject of mirth among many Buddhists I know. "What's with all these lists?!" they cry. If you delve into the Pali Abhidharma, you will find list upon list and even lists of lists! Memorization is facilitated by lists, and since Early Buddhists had a preliterate culture, without memorization it was impossible to transmit information. Even after literacy spread, it was very difficult to reproduce and transport texts. These days memorization may not seem so important, since it's so easy to transmit and save information. I think memorization is a wonderful and valuable practice for bringing teachings into our lives. As I mentioned in the introduction, one of the things that inspired me to write this book was reading Thich Nhat Hanh talking about being required to memorize the "Thirty Verses" as a young monk. I encourage you to chant and repeat these verses until you know them by heart. Not so much by mind, but by heart.

Having said all that, I know that most of you reading this will not memorize these verses, nor the fifty-five mental factors contained therein, nor even the eleven in this line of verse. So here's my take: It's not so much about the specific list you're using. There are other lists of beneficial mind-states out there. The main thing is to commit to cultivating a mind that promotes well-being. We can cultivate beneficial states by studying them, talking about them, thinking about them, and by being mindful of them. Perhaps you think some of these mental factors listed here are harmful or are sometimes harmful. Investigate. This is worth doing. Oftentimes semantics becomes the issue and that's fine, if it opens the door to you seeking a way to be well and promote wellness. *Faith* is a word to which quite a few people I know are allergic. Perhaps it's good to investigate what this word means to you and by what definition could it be said to be beneficial—or not. Most importantly, attend to how you feel and your intention, as you consider it. The most important way to cultivate beneficial mental states is by attending to them when they are present. Just knowing the mind that is here is powerful.

The kind of knowing that I'm talking about is the knowing of mindfulness, which is characterized by a lack of desire and aversion, just seeing. It's not about changing or controlling what it knows. It's characterized by energy, tranquility, equanimity, and nonviolence. It is just being with what is, with nothing extra. Mindfulness of mind is in itself a beautiful expression of the beneficial mental factors.

12

Being with Suffering

The afflictions are desire, aversion, delusion, pride,
wrong view, and doubt.

The secondary afflictions are anger,
hatred, hypocrisy, malice, envy, selfishness, || 12 ||

An excellent way to alleviate suffering is to attend to it in an intimate, nonjudgmental, compassionate manner. Running away from it and trying to control it rarely work.

In every mind afflictions arise—mental states that are, cause, or are conducive to suffering. The first of the six afflictions in this verse—desire, aversion, and delusion—are the three central afflictions referred to throughout Buddhist literature. These verses extend this list of afflictions and include a much longer list of secondary afflictions so that we may develop our awareness of the things that arise that are harmful, an awareness that facilitates letting them go.

Many of the items on this list bring up complex, subtle issues that would take at least a chapter to address.

For instance, there are ways in which doubt, pride, or desire could be construed as beneficial. Investigating the semantics of these terms can be worthwhile, but it may be most helpful to just think of these words—in this context—in the way that seems to you to be clearly afflictive. For example, doubt that promotes deep inquiry is good, but doubt that keeps you on the couch all day watching TV, too hesitant to choose any path, is afflictive. These verses on mental factors recommend working with the emotional/volitional contents of mind so that we may be well and so the way we conduct ourselves in the world will be transformed at the root, in the storehouse.

Although these verses emphasize working with mind, I think it would be good to talk briefly about the ethical culture in which they were created, to talk about Buddhist guidelines for conduct.

This text is called "Thirty Verses on Consciousness Only"; the subject matter is working with consciousness. If we look at the Buddhist Eightfold Path, we see a balancing of meditative, consciousness-transforming practices and ethical, compassionate action. These verses don't address the latter subject. It may be that Vasubandhu downplayed it because of his faith that if you focus on cultivating a mind that is deeply attuned to the interdependence of all things and that manifests beneficial factors instead of afflictions, you will act kindly and in a way that benefits everyone. However it's also true that the majority of the audience for this text were probably Buddhist monks and nuns who had taken vows to follow an extensive list of precepts— not to kill, steal, lie, praise themselves, etc.—so he may not have found it necessary to discuss the subject any further. We still vow to follow these precepts as part of Zen training at my place of practice, and most practice centers encourage following them as well. Although I support this text's emphasis on working with mind, let's not forget that just making a commitment to act kindly and not harmfully, no matter what the mind is doing, is very helpful.

In fact, this kind of commitment integrates perfectly with practicing mindfulness of afflictions. When we are mindful of an affliction. we have the opportunity to choose whether we act on it or not. If we are not aware of our afflictions, we are likely to act impulsively. Then we are mere repeaters of our karma. Let's suppose you have a sister who is more successful in her career than you, and your mother loves to talk about it. You find yourself mentally chewing on things your mother said: "Her bathroom is the size of your bedroom!" Perhaps you utter sarcastic barbs while cooking Thanksgiving dinner together; or you work yourself way too hard at your volunteer job to prove you're better; or you lie around in bed all day, because what's the point, you'll never be good enough. If we are mindful of the afflictions, we can see envy, malice, hypocrisy, restlessness, and laziness arising in the moment; we can see them *as* afflictions, that is to say, suffering. We can observe them with an open heart and mind and watch them pass away without acting on them. This is how we take care of ourselves in the moment, step into responsibility for our own lives, transform our mind so it can be more well, and choose to act in a way that is beneficial rather than harmful.

In the Anguttara Nikaya Buddha is quoted as saying, "Actions willed, performed, and accumulated will not become extinct as long as their results have not been experienced." Remember that Buddha, in another text, defines karma as intention and that intention, in this context, is closely linked to emotion. If you experience envy you will never let go of the habit of envy until you actually have directly and intimately experienced it as itself, not the mental projection it creates. We must taste the feeling, instead of just believing the story, the mental projection that mind makes out of it. This allows the seed of affliction to bear fruit and exhaust itself while we watch, but not create more seeds of affliction. Mindfulness is the practice of this direct and intimate experience, and mindfulness of afflictions is a wonderfully effective means to let go of the tendency to experience the same afflictions over and over again. It is how we can truly let go. As Zen monk Shitou says in "The Song of the Grass-Roof Hermitage": "let go of hundreds of years and relax completely." By seeing ourselves how we are right now, we can let go of the bondage of the past, of our karma.

13

Taking Care of Suffering

Deceitfulness, guile, arrogance, harmfulness,
lack of conscience and humility, sluggishness,

Restlessness, lack of faith, laziness, carelessness,
forgetfulness, distraction, and unawareness. || 13 ||

Like some modern psychological methods, Buddhist practice sometimes encourages us to consciously draw difficult emotions into our mind and body. By allowing ourselves to experience afflictions in the light of mindfulness and our commitment to the alleviation of suffering, we can directly experience the fruits of afflictive karma and let it go. Even including this list of afflictions in this text is an example of this approach; when one reads this list, it probably takes the mind to a darker place than it was before. This list is here to help us face the difficult things that we'd like to avoid or blame on someone else.

Stories actually serve, in part, this purpose of bringing afflictions into our mind. In most cultures, stories include challenges or difficulties, and when we hear them we may experience fear, anxiety, or anger, as well as joy, tranquility, and laughter. Just look at the anxious faces of young children being told the story of Little Red Riding Hood, as she sits on the bedside with the malicious and deceitful predator. How many tissues have been soaked during viewings of the movie *Brokeback Mountain*? We have these stories in some part because we need to know that we are not alone with our pain, that someone else is crying as the aged, fading King Lear rages at his loving, devoted daughter.

Many stories from the Buddhist canon—particularly those from the *Therigatha*, the record of the first order of nuns—tell of terrible sufferings. I vividly recall one retreat in the steep, lush hills of Southern Minnesota where my teacher Tim Burkett told the story of the unbelievably bereft Patacara. She lost her children and entire family in a series of shocking tragedies, and she eventually made a commitment to practice and became one of the great teachers of her time. I wept copiously, my heart cracked wide by hours of meditation, the power of the story, and my teacher's gift for storytelling. I tasted the raw pain of her loss as my own. I saw it in my own consciousness. I left that retreat with an opened heart, a newfound knowledge of my capacity to be with my own suffering, and a deepened sense of the vastness of my connection to all of life through the bond of shared grief.

Stories of course only go so far at helping us be well. Although they allow us to sense, generally unconsciously, that we are not alone with our pain, most of us don't attend too closely to the experience of the affliction that arises; we tend to focus on the story. In order to see the ultimate benefits of drawing into mind the difficulties of life, we need to do it in the context of our vow to end suffering and with our attention focused on actually seeing the painful states as they arise in our mind and body. We need to practice right mindfulness.

Three Buddhist practices that are particularly popular in the United States these days center on cultivating beneficial mind-states but include this method of bringing up and clearly seeing afflictions. The first, the five remembrances, is a series of phrases centering on impermanence and the power of karma:

I am sure to become old; I cannot avoid aging.
I am sure to become ill; I cannot avoid illness.
I am sure to die; I cannot avoid death.
I will be parted from all that is dear and beloved
to me.
Actions are my possessions, actions are my
protection, actions are the womb from which
I have sprung. I am heir of my actions;
as I do so shall I become.

By saying these while practicing right mindfulness, we will likely feel the pang of loss, taste what we would like to push away, see that we can actually be present to that suffering without running away or trying to control things, sense the universality of our predicament, and hence become more compassionate to suffering wherever it arises.

The second is loving-kindness meditation (*metta*). For this practice we think loving phrases about people to cultivate a mind that loves, that manifests beneficial mental factors. However, when doing loving-kindness practice, we often see the mind making afflictions, particularly when we are encouraged to think loving thoughts about people we don't like. We get to see that when anger and judgment arise they are our own suffering. They are ours to take care of.

The third is giving and taking, or *tonglen*. With giving and taking practice, we breathe in the suffering of others and breathe out well-being. We taste afflictions and we see how our aversion to them cuts us off from others; we see how letting them arise and pass away in the light of a mindful heart committed to the alleviation of suffering frees us from our aversion and opens up a vast compassionate connection.

We may have plenty of suffering in our lives already, but if we have a stable base of practice and will not be overwhelmed, drawing up the difficult tendencies of our minds in the warm light of our meditative awareness can allow us to directly know and let go of old conditioned fears, resentments, and barriers.

14

Not Always So

Remorse, sleepiness, initial thought, and analysis
can be either afflictive or not. ‖ 14 ‖

The truth of this verse is not hard to see. Sleepiness
is good when you're in bed at ten o'clock at night. It's
not so good when you're driving a car. Remorse can
be really helpful, for instance, when it provides some
energy and impetus for us to not continue the same
kinds of harmful actions over and over again. If I get
frustrated with my son and say something sarcastic,
a little remorse will help me to be more attentive to
my frustration in the future and careful not to speak
impulsively. However, remorse can also be toxic. There
are things I've done that I thought about and suffered
over and over again for years without making any effort
to change the patterns of thought, feeling, and behav-
ior. I spent most of my twenties in a cage of remorse
and shame that kept me confined, alone, and completely caught in my own conditioned patterns. It took
a comprehensive commitment to my well-being for me

to pick up the key that was sitting in that cage with me, open the door, crawl out, and finally stand up and walk into the evening light.

Initial thought and analysis can be similarly afflictive or not. If you wake up and think, "I will offer myself today to the possibility of universal well-being," I think that's beneficial. If you are singing a soothing sleepy-time song for your baby and you suddenly, anxiously think, "I have way too much work to do tomorrow," that initial thought is probably not helping anyone. Analysis is tricky. My advice is to pay attention, learn to discern whether the way you are analyzing is helpful or not. For instance, we often use analysis to try and mask the pain of experience. Instead of feeling the emotional sting of another's comment, we spend a lot of time thinking about what we should have said in response, trying to judge the other person's motivations, or figure out how to control him or her. This is very rarely helpful. However, if two organizations want to partner to provide food for people with very low incomes, if you want to organize a party for a loved one's birthday, and if this book is to reach your hands, analysis is beneficial and necessary.

It is common and reasonable for people to argue that some, many, or even all of the mental factors listed by Vasubandhu as beneficial or afflictive can actually, like the four in this verse, be both, depending on the circumstance. As I've said, I'm not going to give an explanation of each of the fifty-five factors in this text. However, I will briefly address those that seem to create the most debate: faith and doubt.

Faith is listed by Vasubandhu as beneficial. But it seems to me that if faith means believing ideas or ideologies for which there is no evidence and holding fast to those beliefs, it is harmful. Unquestioning faith in an ideology is what we would call "wrong view"— Mahayana Buddhism emphasizes this, over and over again—and wrong view is indeed one of the afflictive factors in this text. Instead, let me suggest that faith here means trusting that the alleviation of suffering is possible and a feeling of trust in things, as they are, beyond any ideas, conceptions, or ideology you may have. This faith is about trusting what is, and also believing that it is worthwhile to make your best effort in this moment for the benefit of everything.

Doubt, an afflictive factor, refers to a kind of hopelessness and anxiety: a loss of the sense that your effort has any value for the promotion of well-being, and an underlying fear or unease with the way things are. It is an underlying doubt that leaves so many people glued to their computer screens playing games, or constantly refreshing the same pages, trying to distract themselves from a vague unconscious disquiet, and squandering the amazing opportunity of this moment. Of course, doubt, if it means questioning things, can be very helpful. It's clear that Vasubandhu believed this; he devoted his life to questioning, investigating, and refining the ways of thinking about things that he deemed most beneficial. In his later years, he left his commitment to pure Abhidharma thought, of which he was a great and recognized master, and found a way to bring it together with the unknowability of the Mahayana view of wisdom. But this kind of doubt is actually faith; imagine the kind of faith it would take for the pope to become a Unitarian, or for the great cellist Yo-Yo Ma to start singing for a punk rock band—this is the kind of "doubt" that Vasubandhu embodied.

We will see as we enter the second half of Vasuban-dhu's work that all these dualities are not ultimately true, that faith and doubt, remorse, anger, and nonviolence are all just names we create that don't really show us reality. Whether we call what's in your mind this moment afflictive or beneficial, it is always an inseparable part of the vast, unknowable unfolding, beyond good and bad, just-as-it-is-ness. However, Vasubandhu and the Early Buddhist texts we have agree that these names and distinctions can help us shed the patterns that keep us bound in suffering. So think about them and use them, but hold them with some lightness.

15

The Water and the Waves

The five sense consciousnesses arise on the root
consciousness together or separately,

Depending on conditions, like waves
arise on water. ‖ 15 ‖

For the last several verses Vasubandhu has been teaching about the six sense consciousnesses; here and
in the next verse he divides these six into mind and
the remaining five senses: eye, ears, nose, tongue, and
touch. This verse is about the relationship between
this moment of sensory data and the store consciousness, which he calls here the root consciousness. What
Vasubandhu points to here, and expands upon in verse
17, is the notion that what we see, hear, smell, taste,
and touch, and what we generally believe to be the raw,
inarguable facts of existence are, in fact, deeply conditioned by our karma. He gives us a classic metaphor to
apply to our sensory experiences: they are individual
waves and are simply manifestations of the ocean. The
Lankavatara Sutra states, in Francis Cook's translation:

Just as the ocean encounters the condition of wind and produces many waves, but rolls on uninterrupted, so it is with the ocean of alaya battered by the wind of objects and perpetually producing the waves of various consciousnesses . . . rolling on uninterrupted just as it is.

Shunryu Suzuki uses a metaphor of a movie and a screen to beautifully relate the idea that the five senses arise on the root consciousness. What we take to be reality is like a movie, but we are generally unaware that there is a screen. He says, "If you want to enjoy the movie, you should know that it is the combination of film and light and white screen, and that the most important thing is to have a plain, white screen." If your screen is smudged, the movie will be colored as well. The path laid forth by Vasubandhu is one where the karmic processes in the storehouse are overturned at their root, where they create no obscurations, where the root consciousness is made into a plain white screen. This verse is about knowing that there is a screen—an important step.

Have you ever been in a lengthy, heated argument and been able to distinctly recall someone saying something that they now categorically deny they said? We can perhaps chalk such disagreements up to people being disingenuous or to failures of memory, but even in the moment, our senses are not giving us facts but conditioned impressions. In a celebrated recent experiment, subjects were invited to test their concentration by counting the number of passes made by a group of people throwing a basketball in a short film. Many people were able to accurately count the number of passes, but, amazingly, large numbers of them did not notice a person moonwalking across the middle of the screen in a bear suit. When asked afterward about it, they'd deny it ever occurred! Their concentration on the ball completely obscured a moonwalking bear. Surfers see variations in water I can't even see when they explain them to me. Americans briefly shown a series of photographs of people of holding either a wallet or a gun are often mistaken about what is in the person's hands, and they are much more likely to think black people are holding guns when they are not. We do not see the world; we see a projection of the interaction of our senses, our mental conditioning, and, perhaps, some ultimately unknowable external conditions.

Remember though, that Vasubandhu and Buddhism in general are pragmatic. This teaching is not about denying that external reality exists. It is about understanding what and how we know for the purpose of helping us to cultivate and manifest the intention to alleviate suffering. Vasubandhu says the five senses arise like waves on the water of the root consciousness. A sailor who ignores the waves is going to be in deep trouble. It's good to attend to the waves and engage in discernment. If you see charcoal clouds massing on the horizon and the wind is starting to whip up from the East, get inside, or get a raincoat. If you see a red flush forming on your colleague's cheeks and her voice is rising in tone, volume, and pace, attend to what she is saying, how she feels, and your own emotions and thoughts arising. These waves are here in the moment and they are a part of what we are encouraged to attend to mindfully in these verses.

We are also encouraged to attend to the ocean, to the fact that the waves are part of a vast, unfolding inter-dependence, deeply manifesting our past conditioning by creating our present-moment way of seeing. If you see a coconut falling out of a tree toward your head, of course, there's no need or time to direct your attention to the ocean—just get out of the way! However when you feel anxious or threatened at work or at home, it can be very helpful to remember that what you believe to be real, true sensory information about a threat is also a manifestation of your habits of seeing. This awareness—of the screen, the ocean, the storehouse—is here to help us lighten up a little bit, to soften, to have some compassion for ourselves, conditioned beings, to help us see the vast power our conditioning, and find compassion and openness about everything. This is a common thread in Buddhist teaching. Here we are encouraged to see that even at the very most raw and apparently "real" level of our experience—sight, sound, smell, taste, and touch—what we experience is deeply, karmically conditioned. Ultimately, we do not know what is.

16
On Thinking

Thought consciousness always manifests except in the realm of no-thought,

The two thought-free meditation states, unconsciousness, and thought-free sleep. || 16 ||

This verse marks the end of Vasubandhu's explication of the eight-consciousnesses model. As he did with his teachings on the store consciousness and manas, he ends his description of the six sense consciousnesses by explaining the conditions in which they are not found.

This verse deals with some technical aspects of Abhidharma thought. Since my purpose in this book is to focus on how these verses show us a way to practice, I will give a brief explanation and move on.

We have translated the term *mano* as "thought consciousness" here, which in this case is not used to describe a series of words in the mind. It is often called "mind," "awareness," or "knowing." Vasubandhu's understanding is partly based on the Early Buddhist model of the eighteen *dhatus*, or realms, in which there are six sense organs, each accompanied by a sense consciousness and a sense object. This makes six sets of three, a total of eighteen dhatus. There is eye, eye consciousness, and object of sight; then ear, ear consciousness, and sound, etc. Where things get confusing is with mind.

Our old friend manas, in this case, is the mind, the sense base. Mano is thought consciousness, and the sense objects are what we usually think of as thoughts—

EIGHTEEN DHATUS		
Organ / Sense Base	Consciousness	Sense Object
Eye	Eye Consciousness	Sight
Ear	Ear Consciousness	Sound
Nose	Nose Consciousness	Smell
Tongue	Tongue Consciousness	Taste
Body	Body Consciousness	Touch
Manas	Mano / Thought Consciousness	Thought—and all the other sense objects

and the objects of the other five senses. Recall that in verse 5, *manas* is defined as "consisting of thinking." Mano, thought consciousness, functions as a kind of aggregator of what appears in the six consciousnesses. When you are practicing meditation and you are aware of light flickering on the wall, the sound of wind, and thoughts about needing to mow the lawn, each of those things you are aware of is a mind object, though the light and the sound are also simultaneously objects of their respective sense organs. Mano is that which is aware of the light and wind and thoughts, and manas is the "sense organ" on which that awareness is based. So when we say "thought consciousness," here we're talking about awareness, or what is known in some Buddhist texts as "knowing."

This verse tells us that this awareness, knowing, mind, or thought consciousness always manifests except in a few circumstances: the realm of no thought, the two thought-free meditation states, unconsciousness, and thought-free sleep. Sometimes when we sleep, we dream, which means thought consciousness manifests, but sometimes there is no thought consciousness; this is thought-free sleep. It is also sometimes true that there is no awareness when one is in a coma, under the influence of powerful drugs, or unconscious for some other reason. There are also states of deep meditation where no awareness appears. These are the two specific meditation states that Vasubandhu references here. To be clear, this not does describe a state of meditation where there are no *words* moving through your mind, but there is awareness. Only when there is no awareness at all is one in thought-free meditation.

The reference to "the realm of no-thought" is the only thing in the "Thirty Verses" that sits outside of the realm of twenty-first-century rational thought. This is a plane of existence occupied by beings who have no thought at any time. In Buddhist literature, there are many realms: hells, heavens, the realms of fighting spirits and animals, of humans, as well as the realm of no-thought. It is popular in the modern world to explain these as psychological realms or archetypal realms. If one reads ancient Indian texts, however, it seems quite clear that people understood these as literal realms in which one could be reborn. Although a great deal of the "Thirty Verses" is devoted to working with karma, at no other point do they present anything explicitly pertaining to rebirth. All the teachings in this work, so far, have been perfectly understandable and applicable to practicing to be well and promote wellness in this very life. Yet, there is this mention of the realm of no-thought. I'll leave the subject of rebirth to others and just ask this: If what we're seeing is a projection of our karma and we cannot ultimately know what the "external" world is, as Vasubandhu states, does it really matter whether the realm of no-thought is a separate plane of existence or merely a psychological realm? Either way, this moment is our opportunity to practice for the well-being of the world. If we find ourselves in the realm of no-thought, we may just have to take a break from this noble work and resume when we are reborn where thought manifests. If we don't find ourselves in the realm of no-thought, let's take care of what is here in our awareness.

Wisdom

Wisdom Publications

Please fill out and return this card if you would like to receive our catalogue and special offers. The postage is already paid!

Name

Address

City / State / Zip / Country

Email

Sign up for our newsletter and special offers at wisdompubs.org

Wisdom Publications is a non-profit charitable organization.

17

Projection Only

This transformation of consciousness
is conceptualization,

What is conceptualized does not exist,
thus everything is projection only. ‖ 17 ‖

Now Vasubandhu begins the second half of the "Thirty
Verses," and so also begins his teachings on the means to
overcome the barrier of delusion. Just as his teachings
in the first half on overcoming the barrier of afflictive
emotion centered on being intimately aware of afflictions, these teachings on delusion begin by directing us
to realize the depth and completeness of our delusions.

As we move through these verses, we will see that
central to this process is overcoming the delusion that
there is a self separate from other things, the delusion
of alienation. Recall that in the first verses, Vasubandhu
taught that everything conceived as "self" or "other"
occurs in the transformation of consciousness, and that
this transformation has three aspects, upon which he
elaborates in verses 3–15. He opens this seventeenth
verse by saying that everything he has described in the

previous verses, "this transformation of consciousness," is conceptualization. The Sanskrit word we translate as conceptualization, *vikalpa*, can be taken to mean either the process of conceptualizing or the state of being conceptualized. So here he is saying that this transformation we've been discussing and working with is both itself a process of conceptualization and a thing that is conceptualized. The latter should be apparent; this book has been so far a proliferation of concepts about this transformation of consciousness. The former is evident, if we consider that this transformation of consciousness is the process by which we come to conceptualize things as self or other. It revolves on this central conceptualization: there is a self and there are other things. We could say that what consciousness does is discriminate—another common translation of the word *vikalpa*—but Vasubandhu wants to make this clear: consciousness *is* discrimination. If you look through the previous verses and chapters, you will see that every aspect of consciousness is conditioned by karma to interpret things in a way that is colored by conceptualization.

In the second line of this verse, Vasubandhu makes a bold move. He refutes the existence of everything he spent the previous half of his text explaining. "What is conceptualized does not exist." Since he just used a lot of concepts to explain his model of consciousness, it is conceptualized, therefore it does not exist. For

Mahayana Buddhists this type of statement and this rhetorical approach is not surprising. The *Heart Sutra*, perhaps the most central text in Mahayana Buddhism, focuses, as does this line of verse under discussion, on pointing out that the dharmas of Early Buddhist and Abhidharma practice do not fundamentally exist. Often this type of teaching is explained as a means of helping us to not get stuck on the ideas and practices of our tradition and instead stay mentally flexible. The Buddha famously stated regarding his teaching that it is like a raft; when we make it across the river to the other shore, we should not carry the raft around on our backs, but instead we should leave it behind. This is how Vasubandhu begins the section of his work oriented toward letting go of delusion, by reminding us that the eight consciousnesses model is a useful tool, but it is not to be carried around and made into a burden.

When we say that what is conceptualized does not exist, what does this really mean? A common image in contemporaneous Buddhist texts dealing with this subject is "the horns of a rabbit." We can have a concept of horns on a rabbit. Can you picture them? However the horns of a rabbit are not ultimately real. We can imagine things using the power of our conceptual capacity of mind, but they are not really existing things. Here Vasubandhu is saying that since the entire process of consciousness is conceptualization, it never reaches real things. Everything is the horns of a rabbit. This teaching does not deny your direct experience; it points out that it's just experience, it's not the ultimate truth.

Thus everything is projection only. Everything, the All, our ideas, our feelings, what we see and hear, the sound of the breeze in the trees, the memory of a long-loved cat, the thrum of hunger in the belly, our righteous rage, and our vast compassion—it's all projection only.

"Projection only" is a translation of the term *vijnapti-matra*. The famous school of thought associated with this text is called Consciousness Only, *citta-matra*, and I can see why; Projection Only does not have the same ring to it. But Vasubandhu never uses *citta-matra* in this text, only *vijnapti-matra*. Vasubandhu is precise and careful. He avoids the term "consciousness only" because he knows people might get confused and think he means the universe is made of consciousness or some such unknowable thing. He is saying instead that consciousness is all we can experience and that it is constructed by the habits of conceptualization in that process of consciousness itself. In short, all we really know is that we are seeing projection—projection only.

Lest you start to go down some strange and solipsistic mind-road, let me remind you of the context of this teaching. If we know that everything is projection only and we have the model for working with consciousness presented in the first half of this book, we can have some faith that, through practice, we can transform the processes of consciousness so they produce equanimity rather than anger, nonviolence rather than desire, carefulness rather than laziness, energy rather than sluggishness, humility rather than selfishness. We can transform everything—projection only—so that it is well and it is kind in the here and now.

18

The Process of Consciousness

Consciousness is all the seeds transforming
in various ways

Through mutual influence producing
the many conceptualizations. || 18 ||

I have a memory, quite possibly faulty, of a very old
Chinese text on Consciousness Only, perhaps by Xuanzang, that says, "truly, the store consciousness runs the
whole show." I can't find the text, but the message stays
with me. The degree to which our conditioning colors
experience is profound. Recently I was leading a climb
of a small mountain in the Rockies as part of a med-
itation/backpacking retreat. As we prepared for the
climb, I pointed out our route. The more experienced
members of our group understood the plan, but a few
others clearly could not even see the elements of the
landscape—the gullies, the places where loose rock was
slightly less steep—that I was pointing out. As we were
descending some of us were calmly and happily making
our way down a couloir when I realized one member of
the group was near panic. Where some of us saw a nice

little rock ladder to climb down, he saw a vast chasm opening up over a thousand-foot drop-off. I have been on both sides of this myself; I once crawled in terror across a narrow ridge as my climbing companions jauntily jogged back and forth saying, "This is plenty wide enough to walk on!" Although we would all agree that we were in the same place, our perception of that place was profoundly different due to the conditioning of our mind and the projections it created.

I have already introduced much of the material in this verse earlier in the book, but it's worth a review, and Vasubandhu gives us some more specifics on how our karmic seeds produce experience. First he points out the completeness of the power of karmic seeds:

Consciousness is all the seeds transforming
   in various ways
Through mutual influence producing the many
   conceptualizations.

All these conceptualizations that we've been talking about in the last verse are the fruit of karma, the fruit of the seeds of our mental conditioning. The importance of this statement is twofold: it is a message of humility and a message of empowerment. If we know that everything in our consciousness is a conceptualized projection of our karma, we can be humble about what we know. We can realize that we are born as children of conditioned delusion in every moment. When we are getting really angry, we can remember that everything we are seeing and thinking is not the truth but projection. Likewise, if we know this, we can taste a deep and profound sense of empowerment. Since everything we perceive, experience, or think is a projection of karma, and karma is a product of our intentions, our mental formations, we can devote ourselves to making our best effort to cultivate positive intentions in every moment. We can plant the seeds that will produce more *beneficial* projections. As the seminal Buddhist text the "Five Remembrances" says, in Nyanaponika Thera's translation, "I am the owner of my actions [karma], heir of my actions, actions are the womb (from which I have sprung), actions are my relations, actions are my protection. Whatever actions I do, good or bad, of these I shall become their heir."

This verse also makes explicit some aspects of the operation of the eight consciousnesses. The transformation of seeds is the activity of the store consciousness, so we can paraphrase this verse to say, "Consciousness is the activity of the storehouse producing the many conceptualizations." Manas and the perception of the six senses are what is produced by the karmic activity of the storehouse. They are the conceptualizations. So these seeds produce a sense of self, that there is an *I* here, and since there is an *I*, they produce a sense that there are other things: colors, sounds, tastes, thoughts, attention, volition, etc. If there is an *I*, it by definition creates a sense of *other*.

This process is often described as being like a waterfall, in part because long, long ago some Chinese translators rendered "like a river flowing," from the fourth verse, as "like a waterfall." The phrasing of this eighteenth verse also carries the feeling of the rushing activity of seeds transforming, influencing, producing, and proliferating experience. If we practice meditation we begin to see this—feelings, thoughts, and sensory perceptions rush along unbidden. If we commit to meditation, we may also sometimes see that the production of conceptualizations can slow down; analysis fades away, and the experience of the senses softens and slows. We may see, as did the old Indian monk I wrote about earlier, that although things are calm and kind in our mind, there is still this "residual conceit, 'I am.'" We may come a little closer to the roots of the way our mind makes a world with which it can be dissatisfied.

19

The Ripening of Karma

Karmic impressions and the impressions of grasping
self and other

Produce further ripening as the former karmic effect
is exhausted. || 19 ||

The unconscious stream of conditioning that creates
our experience of this moment surges on. The store
consciousness, the ripening, is ever changing, dynamic.
We cannot know what our mood will be tomorrow
or even in a few hours. In each moment new karma is
created and exhausted. One minute we may be calmly
scrolling through the news on a website, the next feeling rising aggravation at the fact that the next page of
our article won't load. In that moment of aggravation
we feel, whether we know it or not, separate, cut off.
The conditioning that we've been developing since we
were born, to feel annoyed when we don't get what we
want, is dependent on the hard and solid sense that
there is an *I*, which should get what it wants.

Vasubandhu continues with the theme of the on-
rushing, dynamic flowing of the process of the ripening

of karma. In this verse he reminds us of the key Yogacara idea that the center of the problem of human suffering is the split between self and other.

On a few occasions I've found myself flowing through a beautiful yoga sequence, in perfect tune with the motion of my body and breath, when suddenly a thought of some past slight someone did to me comes into my head, and anger rises throughout my body and mind. I thought the karmic effect of my emotional response to that nasty thing my friend said to me years ago was exhausted, but here I am, lost in an internal dialogue and cut off from my body and breath. Countless unknown seeds in my storehouse came together to form furthering ripening in me. When it arises, it's my job to take care of it.

In each moment karmic effects are manifesting: we feel located in a body; there are emotions, tranquility, anger, perhaps joy; there are thoughts; there are beliefs, for example, that God is here, or isn't here, that the shape in the corner of my field of vision is a chair, that time is passing, that some people are evil. These are momentary ripenings of karma. They are the way our conditioning produces our sense of the world as we know it. Their effects appear and are exhausted; however with them come impressions or momentary perfumes. When these impressions, or *vasana*, and manas are present, there will be further karmic ripening; there will be another moment in what we experience as conventional human life. With this way of looking at karmic processes, we can remind ourselves that in this moment we can direct our consciousness toward beneficial intentions and in so doing create beneficial karmic impressions and the condition for a more harmonious life. We have this capacity for liberation from our conditioning.

Let's say you feel angry because your mother-in-law has given a lot of unwelcome advice about your children. There is a lot of karma operating here, but in simplest terms there is karmic ripening of anger, probably accompanied by a lot of thinking, perhaps some long internal arguments. When this anger karma ripens, it produces angry karmic impressions. That, combined with the continuous sense of your existence separate from everything else, produces more angry karma. This means you are likely to feel angry in the next moment, too. More importantly seeds of anger will be produced that will manifest days or even years from now in the form of more anger. Someday, you'll find yourself angrily explaining to your children how to raise your grandchildren or perhaps angrily explaining how your children shouldn't give so much advice. It's a ridiculous web, but we don't have to be caught in it.

The key is mindfulness. If we are really present to our own anger and intimately know the feeling, we create—in the very moment that the former angry karma's effect is exhausted—impressions of nonviolence, tranquility, and lack of desire. We don't have to force the anger to stop—that would be violence. We can observe it in stillness, with tranquility, and we can focus not on desiring to be some other way than how we are, or make someone else be other than how they are, but instead simply be wholeheartedly available to what is: our own aching heart. As a seed of the karma of past angers carried through infinite generations and our entire lives is exhausted, rather than unconsciously creating more angry karma, we can choose to be mindful of our emotions and thus let that seed of painful karma be completely exhausted with no residue. We can put one seed of peace and kindness into the ready soil of this great earth.

As well as pointing out how our practice affects the karmic process, this verse deals with the idea that for karma to ripen, for the process that creates suffering to work, you don't only need karma; you also need to be grasping at the ideas of self and other. This is also known as the twofold grasping, or *graha-dvaya*. It is the impressions of karma *and* the impressions of grasping self and other that produces the further ripening. We should recall that, in Early Buddhist thought, nirvana is the complete cessation of suffering, the point at which karma ceases to function and is exhausted. The end of the "Thirty Verses" is a description of total liberation, centering on the end of the twofold grasping.

Earlier, we were introduced to the manas and the

six senses. The manas, through its continuity, creates the sense of self, and it reflexively creates an "other," the name it gives to the contents of the six senses. So now Vasubandhu describes the tendency of consciousness to create this sense of *I* and *other* as grasping, *graha*. We hold on to this sense, unconsciously clinging in our conditioned way. "Grasping," "clinging," "craving," "holding" are all terms closely related in Buddhist teaching to the root of suffering.

Let me take us back to the two barriers to realization: afflictive emotion and delusion. The Yogacara view is that Early Buddhist teachings emphasize dealing with the first, and so there are countless Early Buddhist texts holding up the value of dispassion and calm, the opposites of affliction. Mahayana teachings focus on delusion and hold up *prajnaparamita*, the perfection of wisdom, as its opposite. Abhidharmists, inspired by the Earliest Buddhist texts, teach that we should see all phenomena, dharmas, appearing in the moment, and that realizing that they are not ourselves is liberation. As Buddhaghosa taught, "There is suffering, but no one who suffers." Mahayanists counter that these dharmas themselves are empty of their own self-nature. As the *Heart Sutra* says, "There is no suffering."

Vasubandhu teaches that grasping self and other is the fundamental problem to be overcome. Once we let go of this grip, we realize that all phenomena are not ourselves, since there's no *I* to see them, and we can see that all phenomena do not have their own self-nature, they are not themselves, since there's no *other*. He reconciles competing views with a teaching that points to the possibility of complete liberation. He will provide more descriptions of what this liberation looks like in the final verses; what we need to know here is that he defines the tendency to grasp or hold on to the idea that there is an *I* that is separate from others as critical to the karmic process. Knowing this, we can turn our minds toward being intimate with our feelings and letting go of the stories our minds create to keep us separate. We can open up to the possibility of deepening our sense of connection to everyone in the world, even those we don't like, to everything that occurs, even our sadness when we see the springtime flowers fall.

20

Three Natures

Whatever thing is conceptualized by whatever
conceptualization

Is of an imaginary nature; it does not exist. || 20 ||

Here Vasubandhu begins his teaching on the Yogacara model for understanding phenomena as
having three natures: the imaginary nature; the
other-dependent nature, and the complete, realized
nature. This model of understanding is designed to
enable us to realize the depth of our delusion; the
completeness of our connection to all the things; and
the dynamism, unknowability, and liberation possible when we realize this delusion and intimacy with
everything.

The imaginary nature of things is our projections and
beliefs. The other-dependent nature of things is their
merely being manifestations of infinite conditions.
The complete, realized nature is beyond all dualistic
views. This doctrine of the three natures has a close
kinship with the more commonly known Mahayana

teachings on the idea of absolute and relative natures, or the two truths doctrine.

When you look at an object, or a person, or an emotion, you can see the three natures in each of these things. Using the example of a tree, for instance, we would say that a tree has many characteristics that you know and understand; it is itself, distinct and separate from other things. This is its imaginary nature; the conceptual habits of your consciousness construct it. Of course, many people would agree about its nature and characteristics, for we have extremely similar conceptual conditioning.

The tree also has other-dependent nature; it is sunshine, seeds, air, earth, rain. The elements upon which it depends are infinite, including every drop of rain that has ever fallen on earth, which are all connected, and your gaze as you look at it, without which it would not be the thing you perceive, and all the infinite conditions that came to create that gaze. We have not even begun to scratch the surface of the tree's dependence on other things.

The complete, realized nature is beyond any conceptions although it excludes nothing. It is not the imaginary, and it is not the other-dependent, and it is not other than them either. In "The Song of the Grass-Roof Hermitage," Shitou says, "The vast inconceivable source can't be faced or turned away from." The complete, realized nature is vast, inconceivable. We can provisionally call it a source because, without it, we could not experience the imaginary nature of things that we take to be reality. It can't be faced or turned away from. It is both beyond grasping and always right here and now.

Perhaps this all seems rather heady: I mean really, it's a tree. Look at it! Actually, just stopping and looking at a tree is a good way to allow the mind time and space to soften and open up to a sense of these three natures. To stop and look at a tree allows the mind to touch something in an intimate way and to relax the pace of trying to figure things out. This can plant a seed of presence, and someday you may see a tree in complete realization beyond and intimate with all your ideas about it and your total connection to and interdependence with it.

To call everything conceptualized by any conceptualization "imaginary," to say that everything we think and perceive is imagination, as this verse does, might seem kind of extreme. However recall that in verse 17, Vasubandhu already wrote that anything that is conceptualized doesn't exist. If it doesn't exist and we think it is real, "imaginary" seems like a good description. This doesn't mean there isn't anything that exists. It means we don't know what things actually are. We don't know because they come through the filter of our consciousness.

It is not recommended that we ignore everything of an imaginary nature. We would starve to death. If you're hungry, please consider responding to the imaginary phenomena of hunger, cupboard, plate, and food, and go have some lunch. The problem is that we are totally out of balance. Most people are completely entranced, mesmerized, and driven exclusively by imaginary phenomena. We believe the thought that occurs to us that a better car is what we really need. We believe the stories we repeat in our minds that we are unlovable, or unrecognized in our genius. We see someone driving aggressively or slowly and *know* that they are a terrible person. We are caught in a dream of dissatisfaction, chasing after our imaginations, powerless as we fall to the ground, or locked in immobility as we try and flee shadowy terrors, ashamed and naked as we struggle to finish an exam for a class for which we are unprepared. To be aware that things conceptualized are imaginary is to be able to realize we are in a dream, profoundly conditioned by our unconscious, and relax.

Countless times I have dreamed I was trying to complete some task but was constantly plagued by impediments and errors, overwhelmed by frustration. Slowly it dawns on me: "This is a dream; I don't actually have to be upset about this." In a passage in a long Prajnaparamita sutra, I recall a section where someone is asked how a bodhisattva responds to realizing that life is just a dream. The answer is "with compassion." The reason given in the sutra is that this realization of life as a dream is balanced with realizing the other-dependent nature and the complete, realized nature as well.

In Vasubandhu's model of practice, our capacity to respond to the dream of life in each moment with compassion is also dependent on the work we do, using the first fifteen verses, with the barrier of afflictive emotion. In this and the next several chapters we will dive into Vasubandhu's model for taking care of the barrier of delusion. We have stepped into this stream by looking at the depth of our delusion, by looking into the imaginary nature. Now, let us look into other-dependence and complete realization.

21

Dependence and Realization

The other-dependent nature is
conceptualization arising from conditions;

The complete, realized nature is the other-dependent
nature's always being devoid of the imaginary. || 21 ||

All things arise from conditions. Rain comes from the accumulation of moisture in clouds, flowers come from seeds, babies come from parents, anger comes from perceived injuries, joy arises from being kind to those we love. If we take time to think about this, the situation starts to seem rather complex. The rain actually comes from the interaction of every particle of air in the atmosphere. If one drop of water forms right above your head, ready to land on your umbrella, it must be conditioned by the air around it, but every particle of the air around it is conditioned as well. Everything has to be operating the way it is for anything to happen. The blooming of one tulip in Belgium is dependent on the accumulation of gases in an orb billions of years ago that began to form our sun, and on unknowable years of human effort, and that's less than a billionth of the things it depends on. As Carl Sagan once said, "If you wish to bake an apple pie from scratch you must first invent the entire universe." We cannot see all the conditions that give rise to anything, unless we can see everything that has ever happened in the entire universe. What we can see, if we see the other-dependent nature, is a conceptualization of those conditions. This statement has a twofold meaning, with some practical applications.

Many Buddhist teachings encourage us to conceptualize the other-dependence of things. To think of a cup as being empty of cup nature, for instance, because it is entirely composed of non-cup elements—human ingenuity, sunshine, water, electricity, sand—is to conceptualize other-dependence. I highly encourage you to do this kind of practice. When you see that your child is angry and frustrated, perhaps take a moment to think of all the conditions that arise to create this suffering person in this moment. When you are in the grocery store, take time to contemplate all the things that come together so that you can lift an apple into your basket. When you recall that countless people worked together to bring this piece of food to you, I hope you may taste some appreciation and connection. When you see that emotions and harmful actions come from a vast history of human suffering, I hope that you may feel some compassion for those you might otherwise judge. When you see that your accomplishments are the results of infinite conditions outside yourself, I hope you feel some humility and gratitude.

So it is good to use the mind to think about, to conceptualize, the other-dependent nature. However, Vasubandhu is also saying something deeper and actually a little contentious in Buddhist thought. He's saying that when you *see* the other-dependent nature— when you don't just think about it, but deeply know it—it is still a conceptualization; you have not transcended the operations of consciousness. This is in contrast to many Buddhist texts, generally Mahayana sutras, which suggest that we can completely transcend conceptualization and that it is precisely when we do this that we realize the other-dependence of things. Certainly the other-dependent nature of things can only be seen by a mind much less bound by gross-level conceptions; the other-dependent nature is not the same as the imaginary nature. To truly see the other-dependent nature generally requires a mind trained for years in meditation. To actually see nothing but things free of self-nature and manifesting infinite interdependent harmonious connection is generally the result of long, devoted practice of letting go of mental conceptual habits. However Vasubandhu says that to see this is still a "conceptualization arising from conditions."

Let me illustrate: Many sutras, and many people I know, speak of experience where there is not time—no coming, and no going. As my teacher Tim Burkett said to me rather simply during a face-to-face meeting on retreat where I mentioned to him that time was not apparent to my consciousness, "Time is a concept, and meditation messes with your concepts." It is very hard to describe this state of mind, timelessness, though many descriptions exist. However none that I know of speak of being able to see everything that has ever happened. To realize timelessness does not allow you to see the workers laying the stones for the foundation of the building in which you are practicing meditation, nor to see the space where that building was when it was at the bottom of a great ocean a million years ago; it does not make you omniscient. You can see the infinite connection of everything through practice, you can see through time, but you still see it in this moment, and in the phenomena of this moment: a cup of tea, the sounds of birdsong, the crack of ice melting on a lake in spring.

Consciousness is a momentary phenomena. Infinity is revealed in the phenomena that appear now. As Buddha said, this is the All: sight, sound, smell, taste, touch, and mind. If we contemplate other-dependence, we know that this moment is devoid of self-nature; it is made up entirely of non-moment elements. The human mind is limited to perceiving in this moment, but the fact that there is a moment separate from other things is only a concept. Even when we see the infinite through practice, we see it through the limited lens of the conceptual capacities of consciousness.

"Complete, realized nature" is a translation of *parinispana*. It's a difficult term. Various other translators have called it "the really real nature," "the perfectly accomplished nature," "the absolute," and "the fulfilled own-being." The Sanskrit word carries three principal connotations: wholeness, the way things really are, and what one sees in enlightenment. Our translation of the "Thirty Verses" tries to convey these three using "complete" to express wholeness and "realized" to convey both how things are made real by infinite conditions in the moment and what is seen in realization. Vasubandhu's definition of the complete, realized nature in this line of verse is quite challenging as well. We are entering the realm of the nondual. The logic of nonduality breaks down every possible dualism as it arises—and as a result makes for very confusing statements. Please trust that ultimately it is here to help free our minds. So to dive into what will be one of the more complex passages in this book, let's look at the verse again:

The other-dependent nature is conceptualization
    arising from conditions;
The complete, realized nature is the other-
    dependent nature's always being devoid of
    the imaginary.

The first thing I'll note is that the complete, realized nature is not defined as a "thing"; it is defined as an absence, the quality of the other-dependent nature's always being empty of the imaginary. If we take out the word "always," it can help us work our way toward understanding. Complete, realized nature is the other-dependent without our imaginations or conceptions applied to it. This looks reasonable. What is really real, what the enlightened see, is infinite interdependence with no conceptions layered onto it. This sounds pretty Buddhist to me! Sadly for our minds, which want simple answers, this is only a small facet of what Vasubandhu is presenting.

Let's look again at his definitions of the imaginary and the other-dependent: "whatever thing is conceptualized by whatever conceptualization" and "a conceptualization arising from conditions," respectively. So the complete, realized nature is that "a conceptualization arising from conditions" is *always* devoid of "whatever thing is conceptualized by whatever conceptualization." My friends, I did not bring you here to confuse you. Let's take a breath. The complete, realized nature is that things are always conceptions arising from conditions that are not conceptualized by conceptualization. I'll paraphrase in a much less philosophically precise but hopefully helpful way: enlightenment is a way of seeing that both transcends and is not other than conceptualization. As Zen Master Yaoshan taught, "think not-thinking." In Mahayana discourse, we may speak of going beyond all conceptions to a state of pure nondual awareness where there is only interdependence. Vasubandhu is pointing out that, with this type of discourse, we create a dualism between conceptualization and nonconceptualization. He is encouraging us to realize that conceptualization is not within or without enlightenment. The way our minds work is neither an enemy nor a friend. It is just this. Enlightenment, complete realization, is not somewhere else.

22

The Harmony of Difference and Sameness

Thus it is neither the same nor different
from the other-dependent;

Like impermanence, etc., when one isn't seen,
the other also is not seen. || 22 ||

It would be hard to overstate the importance of the language of nondualism in Mahayana literature, and we see its origins in the earliest Buddhist teachings. In the Samyutta Nikaya, the Buddha teaches that wrong view "depends on duality, upon the idea that things exist and the idea that things don't exist." Countless Mahayana sutras deconstruct dualistic conceptions to point toward a mind that is completely liberated from divisions and separation, a mind that is free and intimate with everything, a mind of infinite compassion. Seeing through dualisms, or seeing their emptiness, is held up as absolutely central to enlightenment. In the *Heart Sutra*, the most widely chanted text in most Mahayana schools, Avalokiteshvara Bodhisattva, the embodiment of compassion, teaches that form is emptiness and emptiness is form. He goes on to say that every sight, sound, smell, suffering, liberation, and thought is exactly not itself. Each thing is no-thing. To realize this is to enter infinite compassion. Like seeing everything we perceive as being imaginary, seeing everything as both itself and not-itself disarms the rigidity of our views and liberates us from the tendency to suffer due to the attachments that grow from those views.

If you find the concept that form is emptiness hard to grasp, that is just fine. The language of nondualism presents an ungraspable vision of the world. If all phenomena are empty of self-nature, there is nothing to hold on to and nothing to reject. There is no ground on which suffering can originate.

Vasubandhu uses nondual language here to describe the relationship between the other-dependent nature and the complete, realized nature. They are neither the same nor different. In Xuanzang's *Chengweishilun*, arguably the most authoritative existing commentary on the "Thirty Verses," he says this: "If they were different, the complete, realized nature would not be the real nature of the other-dependent nature. If they were not different, the complete, realized nature would not be timeless." That things arise dependent on one another is enlightenment. However enlightenment is timeless and things in their other-dependent nature appear only for a moment—they are impermanent. Impermanence and timelessness are not separate. This is true right now of everything you are experiencing.

It is not clear what Vasubandhu is referring to when he says, "Like impermanence, etc." Various commentators provide various interpretations, many of them very confusing (like the rest of this section of the "Thirty Verses"!). When I see a Buddhist text that says "Impermanence, etc.," I think of the three marks of existence taught by the Buddha in his second Dharma talk and referred to extensively throughout his teaching career: impermanence, suffering, and nonself. Vasubandhu says the other-dependent nature and the complete, realized nature are "like impermanence, etc., when one isn't seen, the other also is not seen." When we see that things are impermanent, we see that there is suffering that comes with them, and we see that things don't have a stable, continuous self. When you are on a lovely vacation from your difficult and stressful job, you may not see impermanence. You may forget that this vacation will end, and you may be quite happy; your vacation may seem to be exactly what is real. But it does end, and when you see its impermanence, you may feel let down and miss the bright sand beach, the fruity drinks, and the people waiting on your needs. You will see that the vacation does not exist, it is gone, and then you may feel loss.

Buddha recommends we actually see and deal with these three marks rather than trying to pretend they are not there. He says actually facing them is the road to real liberation from suffering. If we just see that everything in every moment is impermanent, connected to the vast web of human suffering, and empty of self-nature, we can be present to things as they are, in the moment, without trying to hold on to them. We can be present to suffering wherever it arises, with an open heart and without trying to escape from it.

When we see one of these three marks, we tend to see them all. Likewise Vasubandhu teaches that we only see the other-dependent nature if we are seeing the complete, realized nature and vice versa. When we see the infinite, timeless connection of all things in their immediate, vivid, dependently arising nature, we see through our imaginary world.

23

No Own Nature

With the threefold nature is a threefold absence
of self-nature,

So it has been taught that all things have no self. || 23 ||

Many people have critiqued Yogacara teachings for
going against the central Mahayana doctrine of the
emptiness of all phenomena, saying Yogacara claims
that consciousness is a kind of ultimate reality, the only
thing that exists. Others have said it sneakily subverts
the key Early Buddhist doctrine of *anatman*, nonself,
that we cannot locate a lasting self amid everything that
is arising in the moment; they argue that consciousness
is treated in Yogacara as a kind of soul—a self, an atman.
It seems quite clear in reading this verse that Vasubandhu is not forwarding any such views. He says things
have three natures—imaginary; other-dependent; and
complete, realized—and that all of those natures have
no self. No matter how you look at something in this
model of understanding, what you are looking at ultimately does not have an independent, lasting self. This

verse makes very explicit that the three-natures teaching is in accordance with these central tenets of both Early and Mahayana Buddhism.

The teachings of nonself and the emptiness of phenomena are important for many reasons. They reflect the experience of people who have tasted a vast, spacious sense of their connection to all things, the shedding of suffering, and the absence of ultimate truth in anything that comes through the filter of conceptualization. They are also very valuable in keeping the mind supple. According to these doctrines, everything you think to be ultimately true is not. This is incredibly disarming for the mind's habit of creating suffering.

I recall many years ago I was involved in a very difficult and painful relationship with someone, which was characterized by long, furious arguments and even longer protracted periods of aggressive silence. I had been practicing meditation daily and chanting the *Heart Sutra*, that great articulation of seeing the emptiness of all phenomena. I was desperate for a way out of the pattern of suffering in which I was caught. One day we said some things that began to heat into a wrenchingly frustrating argument. My meditation practice began to manifest and I became aware of my bodily sensations. I felt the heat rising to my face and chest, my mind beginning to race. I intimately tasted my own suffering and saw the thoughts zooming by, trying to control my opponent. Suddenly everything fell away. It's rather hard to describe. The angry face of my partner, the painful sensations of anger in my own body, the morning sunlight streaming across the room—none of them were separate from anything. The totality of the connection of all these things to the vastness of human suffering, the complete lack of truly knowing what was really happening, the profound intimacy of everything—all were manifest in a dreamlike sense of things not being themselves, not being what moments before I would have angrily sworn they were. I saw the suffering in that room connected to all of history, and I stopped fighting. I would like to be clear: this is not a description of enlightenment, this is a description of a simple moment in the life of someone dedicated to Buddhist practice.

The material in the first half of the "Thirty Verses" recommends practicing mindfulness of phenomena, particularly the five universal factors and beneficial and afflictive emotions. The later verses, in keeping with their relationship to Mahayana Buddhism's great emphasis on the nondual nature of phenomena, suggest a different kind of practice—one not based on observing an object, which creates a duality.

The idea of practicing nonduality is problematic, since it's kind of hard to know how to do something that already both exists and doesn't exist. For instance, one of the higher states of meditation (*dhyanas*) described in Early Buddhist texts is "neither perception nor nonperception." How does one do that? In the largest body of texts on the subject, the Prajnaparamita sutras, we are not given very clear instructions. In the *Heart Sutra*, we learn that *prajnaparamita* (the perfection of wisdom) is nonduality and that Avalokiteshvara Bodhisattva, by practicing this perfection of wisdom, liberates everything from suffering. We don't, however, get instructions in *how* to practice the perfection of wisdom, how to practice nonduality. Nonduality is, by nature, slippery and ungraspable, but there are some texts that can give us clues on how to practice it.

In Early Buddhist texts, we find two aspects of meditation practice—*vipassana*, or insight, and *samatha*, or calm abiding. They are understood and explained quite differently among the schools of Buddhism. One of the first known Yogacara texts, the *Samdhinirmocana Sutra*, lays them out in a distinctive way that clearly inspired aspects of Vasubandhu's verses. It defines vipassana as the practice of mindfulness of phenomena recommended in the first half of this work and samatha as practicing "the observation of nonconceptual images." The language is hard to parse; given that in Yogacara teachings all things that we can see or know are conceptualized, observing nonconceptual images seems kind of difficult, certainly paradoxical. However if we soften our stance on the definition of what is conceptualized, the *Samdhinirmocana Sutra*'s definition of samatha works pretty well; practice observing what is happening without adding any concepts. Just see what arises, just sit. In vipassana we label or discern phenomena: here is calm, here is envy, here is a volition impulse, etc. In samatha we suspend all judgment and analysis.

Many meditation instructions offer awareness of breath in the body as the basis for samatha; it is surely a good foundation. Just breath. In Dogen's *Universal Recommendation for Zazen*, he begins his meditation instruction thus: "Stop measuring things with thoughts, ideas, and views. Give up the operations of mind, intellect, and consciousness. Do not think good or bad. Do not judge true or false." This gives some good direction in how to practice samatha, but it is still dualistic. For example, we are instructed not to judge, which creates a duality of judging and not judging. We will see this is not the end of Dogen's instruction on the subject, but it's a good place to start. The *Samdhinirmocana Sutra*'s definition of how to practice samatha offers the similar instruction of "observe without conceptualizing," but it also suggests something deeper, something beyond duality, something ungraspable: observing something nonconceptual that is, by definition, conceptualized by the process of consciousness.

The *Awakening of Faith*, a highly influential sixth-century text whose origins are murky but is probably from China, contains many Yogacara ideas. In it there are instructions on vipassana and samatha; here are that text's beginnings of the instructions for samatha practice, in Yoshito Hakeda's translation:

> Sit erect with an even temper. Attention should be neither focused on the breath, nor on any form of color, nor on empty space, earth, water, fire, wind, nor even on what has been seen, heard, remembered, or conceived.

Focus is directed toward nothing. Generally the human mind focuses on a train of thought, or jumps about from object to object. Vipassana meditation gives the mind an object to attend to, on which to concentrate. In the *Awakening of Faith*'s instructions, samatha does not.

What is most striking to me, however, is that the *Awakening of Faith* equates samatha with cessation; it says that to practice samatha in this way is to practice cessation.

Cessation plays a major role in the Buddha's first and most fundamental teaching, the four noble truths: suffering, the origin of suffering, the cessation of suffering, and the Eightfold Path, which leads to the cessation of suffering. Cessation is nirvana, the end of suffering, and it is simply defined as the letting go of craving, of wanting things to be other than they are. Cessation is achieved over time, through practice.

However, many Mahayana teachings say everything is nondual. Therefore, suffering and nirvana are not separate. Enlightenment is now. The *Awakening of Faith* says you can practice cessation now; samatha, nondual meditation, is the practice of cessation. Zen Master Dogen's central message, also, is that we can practice enlightenment right now. How do we do this? Dogen says we should engage in whatever we are doing whole-heartedly: scrubbing toilets, talking to lawyers, eating rice, raking leaves, sitting still, whatever it is, do it with your whole self. We should do it with no object—no goal and no object, nothing that is separate from us. We should practice nondualism. In his *Universal Recommendation for Zazen*, Dogen quotes Yaoshan's teaching on how he rests in steadfast composure, calm abiding, samatha: "I think not-thinking."

Nondualism is paradoxical and impossible to define; language always puts a false limit on it. Nondualism is impossible to practice, but we are always doing it, as we are already completely not-separate from our activity and the whole universe; it is already our complete, realized nature. How do you practice samatha, cessation, how do you practice the radical and complete shedding of the delusion of separateness? There is no answer outside this moment of experience, but we have some clues left by masters along the way. Completely give yourself to this moment without judging or figuring anything out. Everything is included.

24

Three Natures, All Without Self

The imaginary is without self by definition.
The other-dependent does not exist by itself.

The third is no-self nature—that is, || 24 ||

Imagine yourself in a desert. The glare of the sun pushes your eyes down toward the sand, which makes the sweat run, burning, into your eyes. You are heading north to home and family on the shore of the vast, cool ocean. To the west, across the shimmering waves of burning gold you see a pool of water. Relief! You turn your course toward the cool, refreshing sight, but it never seems to get any nearer. With every step it still hovers just along the horizon, and the well of your thirst grows deeper.

The metaphor of a mirage is a classic Yogacara description of the imaginary nature. Something occurs in our senses that we believe to be real, external, and desirable, and we pursue it endlessly. This is samsara. Sure, we may enjoy some of our time in the desert, but we spend a vast amount of our time working for things that don't actually promote our well-being. It's well documented that wealth beyond enough to secure food, shelter, and medicine has almost no bearing on human happiness, yet look how much energy is put into pursuing a little (or a lot) more money. Money is just a concept, an imagination. It does not ultimately exist outside of its dependence on our belief in it. Sure, it's a useful thing to imagine sometimes, and it can be nice to share the imagination and buy lunch for you and a friend, or send some imagination to Amnesty International, but it's not worth overworking yourself just to get a little extra imagination.

Infinite conditions come together to create the appearance of the mirage. Heat, the sun, the horizon, thirst, eyes, desire, molecules of oxygen, and so on. The conditions of an unknowably vast past, the countless components of this momentary experience, and the way our mind conceptualizes—conditioned by family, our actions, evolution, and culture—all participate in this web of dependencies that create the image that appears to be water where there is none. This is the mirage's other-dependent nature.

When we see the other-dependent nature we see that conditions have come together to create the appearance of a thing, and we see the complete, realized nature. We know that the shimmering dark image on the horizon is a mirage, and we are aware that it is a result of infinite conditions working together. If we think about the other-dependence of a thing, we might say, "My thirst, the way my eyes function, the heat, the sand, and the atmospheric conditions are all arising in a way that makes me think that image over there will make everything okay if I can just get to it." We know that the water is not itself, but an image created by dependence. When we see in this way, we can be aware that others will be desiring and striving to get to the water, and our heart will be touched to know that vast numbers of people are worrying, working, and struggling to get to the imagined relief of the shimmering oasis. Instead of being caught by desire, we can be aware of it and see that it arises dependent on everything else. We can turn our attention from pursuing the object of desire, the imaginary water, or the magical wealth, and turn it toward the central work of Buddhism: the alleviation of suffering.

Vasubandhu gives us some help in developing a sense of the complete, realized nature in this and next verse. Here, he says it is no-self nature; to see the complete, realized nature is to see not water, not a mirage. This is an important point for beginning. Enlightenment itself—"the way things appear in enlightenment" is part of the semantic range of the term "complete, realized nature"—is not a thing. It is, by definition, nonself, empty. This means you cannot have it, you cannot hold it. There is not an ultimate reality that you get to see because you are enlightened. This is not something you can grasp or acquire, and within it there is nothing to grasp or acquire.

The term "realize" is felicitous. Complete realization is possible; it points toward a mind that has realized something and also to the act of its being made real. What is realized is neither the same nor different from the other-dependent and has no self—it is not a thing.

25

Four Ways to Express the Inexpressible

The complete, realized nature of all phenomena, which is thusness—

Since it is always already thus, projection only. || 25 ||

Vasubandhu makes one of the more extraordinary statements in this text at the end of this verse. He says that projection only—whatever we are experiencing right now, the illusion created by our karmic conditioning—which presumably this entire text is designed to help us transcend, is identical with complete realization.

In this verse describing the complete, realized nature as being absent of self-nature, he uses a fourfold description: it is nonself; it is complete, realized nature; it is thusness; and it is projection only. Dogen Zenji makes a very similar argument in characteristically poetic fashion in his essay "Painting of a Rice Cake." Although the essay is complex and covers a great deal of ground, it is principally a commentary on an old Zen saying, "a painting of a rice cake does not satisfy hunger," the most common interpretation of which is that the endless craving that characterizes the human condition cannot be satisfied by anything conditioned by our conceptualizations. A painting of a rice cake is not a real edible rice cake; it is of an imaginary nature, it is a projection. This is a major theme in Mahayana Buddhism. We must let go of all concepts to see the emptiness of phenomena and that is how we go beyond birth and death, beyond samsara, beyond suffering, and how we may engage in the world of suffering and be completely available in every moment. This certainly would seem to be a theme of the "Thirty Verses"—to look into the depth of our delusion about the world and investigate the patterns that cause it so that we may let it go. Dogen, like Vasubandhu, investigates thoroughly the necessity of letting go of conceptualization, to see how a painting of a rice cake cannot satisfy hunger. At the end of the essay, though, Dogen writes, "there is no remedy for satisfying hunger other than a painted rice cake." The complete, realized nature is projection only. We do not realize the way by transcending or escaping projection only; we do it by realizing that the no-self nature of everything *is* projection only, complete realization, thusness, just this moment. And it is always already thus.

Thusness, or *tathata* in Sanskrit, is sometimes translated as "suchness." It refers to things right in this very moment, undivided by conception. Or, we might say, it refers to just this very moment, just this. It is an affirmative expression of the concept of emptiness. It is this moment of experience, of consciousness, without an overlay of concepts. We find some sense of what "thusness" refers to when the thinking mind slows way down in meditation and we find ourselves absorbed in simple uncategorized sounds, the patterns of light and dark on the floor, the sensations, unjudged, in the body. The complete, realized nature is right here in momentary concrete sensual experience, in your fingers holding this book, and the plane flying over my head.

In Shitou's poem "Harmony of Difference and Sameness" he says, "progress is not a matter of far or near." The characters translated as "far" and "near" also carry the meanings "transcendence" and "intimacy," respectively. To see the no-self nature of things is transcendence, to realize the complete, realized nature of projection only, of thusness, of your experience right now, is intimacy with our own mind, with everything. Shitou has internalized the message of this verse of Vasubandhu's. He's saying "difference" and "sameness," "near" and "far," are not two. Being completely intimate with whatever is here—joy, tranquility, anger, the sound of traffic, selfishness, lamplight, sleepiness— is the only way to transcendence, and transcendence only occurs in complete intimacy with how things are right now, thusness. You cannot realize the way by trying to escape.

The phrase "always already thus" is striking. Everything is always, already thus: nonself, complete realization, thusness, and projection only. Whatever consciousness is manifesting right now—perhaps a sense that you are a person reading a book in a chair—is simultaneously none of those things, a projection of karma, exactly what it is, and enlightenment. Enlightenment is not something separate from anything else. It is not a thing, but it is the nature of everything, always. The most extraordinary thing about this grand series of paradoxes is that they are merely the best efforts made by people in the Buddhist tradition to describe their experience, which is not their experience, because there is no one there in the middle to experience it. Why bother to describe this, why leap high into these impossible, linguistic hoops? Because they can point us on the way to practice and perhaps they can provide some encouragement along the way for those of us who wish to devote ourselves to universal well-being.

Each aspect of this fourfold description of Vasubandhu's can help us. Studying that the nature of everything is nonself can help us to let go of the rigidity of our ideas, which keeps us feeling separate and caught in our web of self-centered needs created by that sense of separation. Reminders that everything (including you!) is complete realization, is enlightenment, can let a great beam of light into us, a buoyancy, an illumination, a lifting, a softening of our heart, to everything we meet. Teachings on thusness remind us to just be here, in life, right now, exactly as it is. This very moment, however it is and whatever your activity, is your opportunity to give yourself wholeheartedly to the world: Change the diaper, type the report, listen to the radio, hug your mom. Do it with your whole heart. This is the whole thing, complete realization. That everything is always projection only reminds us that we don't know what's real: we are and are in our conditioning, we have our minds and hearts, our own emotional projections, our own habits and conceptions to take care of always. In taking care of what arises in this moment in our six senses, we can take care of our projection only. Every thought and every person, every animal, and every blade of grass is in this projection. They are all, in this very moment, our chance to step into the Way, into the vow to give ourselves to the well-being of the world.

26

How We Are Bound

As long as consciousness does not rest
in projection only,

The tendencies of grasping self and other
will not cease. || 26 ||

Vasubandhu does not here offer us a vision of escape from
our projections and our karma; he offers the possibility
of finding peace right in the midst of them. He is offer-
ing us hope for liberation from the relentless tendency of
the mind to create grasping, and thus to create suffering.
He does this while harmonizing the Early Buddhist idea
that we practice to go from samsara to nirvana with the
Mahayana idea that samsara and nirvana are one.

Nirvana is defined variously in Early Buddhist
texts, but basically it is nonsuffering, the end of desire,
aversion, and delusion. In the *Thirty-Three Synonyms for
Nirvana Sutra*, the Buddha teaches that nirvana is "the
peaceful, the deathless, the sublime, the secure, the
destruction of craving, the wonderful, the unailing,
the unafflicted, dispassion, freedom, nonattachment,
the shelter, the refuge, the destination, and the path

leading to the destination." Here Vasubandhu uses a similar word, *avatiṣṭhati*, which is sometimes translated as "abide" or "rest." This verse says that until we find rest here in projection only, the grasping of self and other will not cease, and thus, the cycle of seeds of suffering will continue. If we let consciousness rest in how things are a little bit, the tendencies of grasping self and other will soften, and some seeds will be planted that may fruit another day in deeper rest and a yet-more-open hand of thought. Many of my friends have talked about how after sitting silently on retreats at our Zen practice center, we often find that we feel a close bond, a deep connection to the other people there, people we may never have spoken to or even looked full in the face. A few days of letting the body be still and allowing things to come and go with an observant but relaxed mind, a few days of just resting in what is, bridged the apparent gulf between ourselves and others.

Vasubandhu is reminding us that getting to nirvana is about going from a place of grasping to finding a place of rest. But in the same sentence, he is also saying that nirvana is not outside of samsara; rest is not outside of the very process of projection only that creates samsara. Rest is not going to be found when consciousness ends, nor when projection only is overcome, but when consciousness rests *in* projection only. He is saying that to realize the Buddha way we must be intimate with and completely realize projection only—that is, whatever is here in this moment. Recall that avatisthati means "abide" as well as "rest"; consciousness always rests in projection only because there is nowhere else for it to be situated. Samsara and nirvana are not separate. Nirvana is "the destination, and the path leading to the destination."

Vasubandhu places the twofold grasping of grasping self and other, *graha-dvaya*, at the very heart of what must be shed if we are to find peace and freedom. If we look back to the nineteenth verse, we will see that this sense of being a self perceiving other things is central to the way karmic seeds are produced:

> Karmic impressions and the impressions of
>   grasping self and other
> Produce further ripening as the former karmic
>   effect is exhausted.

Without karma and this grasping, the cycle that creates our habits of body, speech, and mind that cause suffering does not function. As the Early Buddhists say, when we see that none of the phenomena of the present moment are "self," we find liberation, and as the Mahayanists say, when we see that none of the apparent phenomena of the present moment have a self, we liberate all beings. Vasubandhu says we can realize both these truths by opening the hand of thought, by letting go of the grasping at the root of experience.

27

Thinking About It Is Not Enough

By conceiving what you put before you to be
projection only,

You do not rest in just this. || 27 ||

When I taught my first class on the "Thirty Verses," each week I gave a practice assignment, such as being mindful throughout the day of a specific affliction—for example, envy—or thinking about the other-dependent nature of things we saw by listing things on which they were dependent. On the last week I asked the students to frequently stop to look at things and think, "This is projection only." One student, to my amusement, called this "the universal solvent" of practices, in that it dissolved all phenomena down to one thing: projections of our karma. This is an extremely helpful practice, but it's important to acknowledge, as I did when I gave this assignment, that this verse specifically states that thinking that something is projection only is not realization.

Vasubandhu, in this twenty-seventh verse, tells us that we can't fully be at rest if we are conceiving what we put before us to be projection only. This line is difficult to translate; a couple of interpretations seem reasonable. First it may refer to placing an object in front of oneself as an object of meditation such as a candle, or a statue of Buddha. The meditative practice of concentrating on viewing an object is very old, and Vasubandhu is not saying it's bad. This verse does say that if, through such practice, one arrives at a eureka moment ("It's projection only!") one has not arrived at the profound rest toward which he hopes we will aspire. The line also reminds us that if we are conceiving of something as projection only, we ourselves have in fact put it there in front of us by conceiving it. Our "realization" that it is a projection only is a projection only.

In the last verse Vasubandhu intimated that "consciousness resting in projection only" was a key to realization, or a way to describe settling into a vast sense of connection. Here he says that as long as we're conceiving objects in front of us we won't "rest in just this." A more literal translation for *tanmatra*, which we translated as "just this," might be "thus only." In projection only, thus only, just this, whatever this is, this moment, or these phenomena, we can rest. We don't need to wait for some different, more appropriate phenomena to arrive so we can come to complete peace. There's no doubt that most people who have talked about this profound state of rest have spent lots of time living in silence, in seclusion, in stillness, practicing meditation, but many of them have realized the deepest peace in the oddest of circumstances, like the nun Dhamma, far back in Buddha's time, who practiced for years until she was very old and infirm. She was walking with a cane and fell down, and suddenly, in her words, "my heart was freed." Monks have found peace as their teachers startled them with shouts or asked them impenetrable questions, and Basho points to realization at the scent of plum blossoms on a sun-and-fog-drenched springtime hill. We may or may not find some great awakening, but we can rest in just this. We can rest in whatever circumstance is here.

We can cultivate resting in just this by practicing mindfulness of the breath in the body. In the *Thirty-Three Synonyms for Nirvana Sutra*, Buddha says that the way to realize nirvana is to practice mindfulness of breath, and then he encourages his monks to meditate at the roots of trees and in empty huts. If we attend to the breath without any judgment or need to control, we may then begin to, as the *Samdhinirmocana Sutra* says, "meditate on a nonconceptualized object."

As the mind rests on the breath without judging it, it may begin to rest on whatever is happening, not holding or understanding, but simply resting in just this. This resting may begin to permeate life. When fireworks come, we can rest in fireworks. When we get a promotion, we can be at rest in good news. When illness comes we can be at rest in the suffering. The fact that everything is projection only does not diminish the fact that right now, there is just this. This moment beyond any understanding we can ever have is the opportunity for us to give our heart and our effort to how things are, to give ourselves to complete realization, and as Zen Master Shitou says to "let go of hundreds of years and relax completely," to rest in just this.

28

Being at Rest

When consciousness does not perceive
any object, then it rests in projection only;

When there is nothing to grasp,
there is no grasping. || 28 ||

How can one describe enlightenment? Dongshan answered, "Three pounds of flax"; Mazu said, "This very mind is Buddha"; Gutei held up one finger. So many people for so many years have written or spoken of it, and most would also point out that the description is not the reality. As the old saw says, when the Buddha points toward the moon, do not confuse the finger for the moon.

In the last three verses, Vasubandhu offers a description of enlightenment. He starts here by giving what Yogacarins view as the key to understanding how enlightenment occurs; realization, he says, occurs "when consciousness does not perceive any object." This does not mean attaining some infinite blackness, although the near-mythical founder of Zen, Bodhidharma, did describe the highest truth as "a vast emptiness." What

Vasubandhu is talking about is a moment of consciousness where there is nothing "other," a moment where the afflicted manas is not dividing experience into self and other. You may have experienced some profound state in your life where you were so focused that your sense of self was weakened, or even gone: perhaps while playing music or sports, or attending to a child. But even in these moments manas still probably had a part in the way your mind was functioning. I believe Vasubandhu is speaking here of a very profound and total alteration in how consciousness works. When consciousness does not perceive any object, there are not "things." The reason that this is a place of "rest in projection only" is that if there are no things, there is no need for a self to try and manipulate them. "When there is nothing to grasp, there is no grasping."

This verse exemplifies the description of enlightenment that has caused many doctrinal disputes among Buddhists over the years. I have generally avoided talking about these philosophical matters in this book, but I'll briefly address them here. If we look at this verse, Vasubandhu is saying that in enlightenment there is consciousness resting in projection only. Early Buddhist texts show the Buddha teaching that all phenomena are empty of a lasting, independent self; *all* phenomena are empty, including consciousness. The *Heart Sutra* clearly states that consciousness is empty and that realizing this emptiness is key to enlightenment, to the realization of the bodhisattva's vast compassion. Over the years many have argued that Vasubandhu is claiming that there is one thing that is ultimately real: consciousness. I will offer two comments. First, Vasubandhu makes no such claim. He says consciousness, like all things, has three natures: imaginary; other-dependent; and complete, realized (which is nonself). Our ideas about consciousness are imagination; whatever it appears to be, it is something arising from conditions, and it is ultimately devoid of self-nature, of a lasting, independent self. Second, I will say that many Consciousness Only texts, although realizing this, argued that consciousness *is* here now. The reason for such an argument is twofold: They first contend that the people arguing with them are stuck on their idea that everything is empty, a fixation which the great genius of the doctrine of emptiness Nagarjuna called the ultimate sickness. They next point out that if there's no consciousness, if there is nothing here, no projection, with what and why would we argue?

The argument that Vasubandhu's vision of consciousness with no object resting in projection only could cause people to think that consciousness is some kind of ultimate reality is one that we should take to heart. There is a real danger that someone studying this material will think that they can develop some ultimately real consciousness that knows an absolute truth no one else knows. In fact perhaps the most quoted line from the *Samdhinirmocana Sutra* is "I do not teach this [Consciousness Only] to ordinary people, fearing they will grasp it as a self." This is a confusing teaching and people can be confused. I heartily pray that my efforts in working with these teachings help people find a way toward peace and harmony.

If we review the early verses of Vasubandhu's text, in verse 7 we see that manas is not found in enlightenment or the bodhisattva path, the states this twenty-eighth verse describes. However the six senses do not cease to function in these states. If we review Vasubandhu's explanation of the contents of the six senses, we find the universal, specific, and beneficial factors, the afflictions and secondary afflictions. It is not stated in this text but it is assumed that one is not likely to reach the state of enlightenment without training the mind to manifest beneficial rather than afflictive emotions. As we cultivate and begin to manifest humility, lack of desire, lack of aversion, lack of delusion, energy, and equanimity, and we let go of pride, anger, envy, laziness, and distraction, the mind begins to rest in how things are, and consciousness softens into the capacity to rest in projection only.

So this mind with no object is one that is manifesting beneficial emotions as all six senses are operating, but without seeing any of them as being self or other, and without any afflictive emotions arising from its own karma. However, in any moment, there is likely to be affliction in this consciousness for there are what would be conventionally understood to be *other* people. There is a vast ocean of afflictive emotion in this world, and the consciousness that has no object, that is completely at rest, does not see these afflictions as self or other. They are simply here, just this. Thus this consciousness naturally moves due to its tendency to manifest beneficial emotions, to help where affliction arises. It doesn't move to try and control an "other" thing, or fix another person. It simply moves, in this very moment, in the way that is most beneficial, like someone adjusting a pillow in the night.

This model of enlightenment can show us a way of being in this world that is completely devoted to peace, harmony, and ease for everyone, forever. It can orient our heart to the possibility of giving each moment to alleviating suffering wherever it is. Self and other are merely imaginary, though conventional and often useful, projections, but arising within the six senses, there is the possibility of manifesting beneficial mind. If you are angry, be present to your anger. If someone else is angry and you are not overcome by reactivity, you can be present to their anger. If you are in danger or overcome with afflictions, do what is most beneficial. This is a model that shows us we can send some money to help impoverished farmers to dig a well while we let go of the paralyzing desire to overcome all of world hunger. We can devote ourselves to a political cause, and if we lose, we don't have to feel beaten or burned out, because there is not an "other" that we are trying to change. We are simply manifesting our beneficial emotion in action right now. We can let our children know that we think they are cultivating a harmful habit by staring at their smartphone several hours a day, but we can let go of trying to be in control of them. We can rest in the way things are, rest in our projections, rest in the awareness that all the habits, all the karmas, in the world are absolutely and intimately connected. All of our suffering, all of everyone's vast and beating hearts, all our love and compassion arriving here, right now, with no other.

29

Transformation at the Root of Suffering

Without thought, without conception,
this is the supramundane awareness:

The overturning of the root,
the ending of the two barriers. || 29 ||

The awareness of the bodhisattva, the "supramundane awareness" mentioned here, is a knowing that does not perceive an other. It is knowledge without an object, with nothing to grasp. This is not a thought or an idea; thoughts and ideas are things that are separate from other things. Vasubandhu swims out with us again into the vast, inconceivable ocean of nondualism, playing in a sea of language where we may perhaps glimpse something beyond our ordinary, mundane view. Here in the warm waters, we do not know if we are the ocean or the waves. We may simply, calmly flow in this not-knowing.

The first line of the verse points to nonduality in a couple of ways. First, the term "supramundane awareness" is a translation of *jnanam lokottaram*. *Jnana* is usually translated as "awareness" or "knowledge." A related term, *vijnana*, is generally translated as "consciousness." That prefix *vi-* is closely related to the English prefix *di-*, as in dichotomy, or divide. It's significant, then, that Vasubandhu uses *jnana* rather than *vijnana*. The knowledge of the bodhisattva does not contain the self/other split that characterizes our mundane knowledge; it is undivided. It is not *vi-jnana*, dividing consciousness, but *jnana*, direct knowing with no self or other.

However there is a problem with the idea that we can train our minds to directly know what is real, to have this supramundane awareness: the afflicted manas may just creep back in and we might think that we know the Truth with a capital T. Thinking we know Truth has caused a lot of problems in our long-suffering human world. So this line reminds us that the bodhisattva's direct knowledge is without thought, without conception; it is not-knowing.

The supramundane awareness that can be realized through this path is not omniscience. It is just this, it is thusness. In Zen practice we put great emphasis on attending to just this, whatever this moment is. Actually we are often given the instruction not to *attend* to just this, but instead actually *just this*, without someone attending and without an "it." This is the practice of immediately entering the supramundane path, for the bodhisattva is not other than just this. Right now. Just this. Look up!

In practicing just sitting, or perhaps mindfulness of breath, or mindfulness of emotions, or any kind of meditation practice, it is very common to find ourselves in a fight with thoughts. We think if we could just get rid of these pesky thoughts, we can finally get down to some real meditation. It is true that many meditation practices include and benefit from the gradual resting of the tendency of mind consciousness to relentlessly produce thoughts. So we might think that, since this line is about the bodhisattva's knowledge being without thought, as soon as thoughts stop, we'll be enlightened. This line, however, points to a nondual relationship between thought and nonthought.

In the earlier verses Vasubandhu tells us that store consciousness is overturned in enlightenment, and afflicted manas is not found in enlightenment, but thought consciousness always manifests, except in a few particular states of mind, none of which are enlightenment. Enlightenment, according to these verses, is both with and without thought. If we cannot conceive of this, that is good, for it is inconceivable. Why is inconceivability good? Because it cannot be grasped. Feel free to open the hand of thought.

The overturning of the root, sometimes called "transformation at the base," is a major theme in Yogacara Buddhism. It is the point at which the entire karmic process in the store consciousness is transformed. When the mind does not perceive an object, when there is nothing to grasp and no grasping, the ancient conditioned habitual tendencies of consciousness are transformed. The storehouse is transformed from being the place or process whereby our conditioning manifests and is stored, into a vast mirroring wisdom that directly knows and shows the world. Rather than seeing a person of a different race in front of us through our lens of accumulated prejudice, we may simply see their humanity, their infinite connection to ourselves. Rather than seeing a hard rain that soaks our clothes as we walk home in an unpredicted downpour in terms of our aversion to the experience, we may deeply experience the wet of the clothes, the chill in the body, the thoughts in the mind, and the scowls and wry smiles on faces passing by with no judgment. The store consciousness transformed at the root, the great mirror wisdom, does not taste the moment in terms of a self with needs, but as a vast, unknowable, infinitely connected thusness.

This is the ending of the barriers of afflictive emotion and delusion. When there is nothing to grasp, there is no ground for selfishness, aversion, carelessness to stand on. The delusion that there is an *I* apart from this thusness in this moment, apart from the infinity of unknowable conditions, apart from those we might love, hate, try to control, or ignore, evaporates like steam from a mirror.

30

The Blissful Body of Liberation

It is the inconceivable, wholesome, unstained, constant realm,

The blissful body of liberation, the Dharma body of the great sage. || 30 ||

Consciousness that rests in projection only, that sees no object, is the knowledge of the bodhisattva, and according to this last of the thirty verses, it is an inconceivable, wholesome, unstained, constant realm, as well as the blissful body of liberation. Vasubandhu has described enlightenment many ways in this text: being at rest in what is, nonseparation from anything, knowledge beyond thought. In this verse he describes it as a place and a body. Although the language is lofty, and the concepts in the "Thirty Verses" are complex, finally Vasubandhu describes the ultimate goal of the Buddhist path as being right here now where we are in this body, where all practice begins and ends.

If all we had of these descriptions of realization was the first line of this verse, we might think that practice was designed to take us to another realm. However, in the last three verses of this work, Vasubandhu gives us a variety of ways to describe realization. We might be able to focus on one briefly and believe it to be the most real or important one, but if we sit and look awhile we will see that, like the facets of a jewel, none of them exists without the other, that what we see and how we describe it are totally dependent on how we look and how the light is shining.

This realm is inconceivable by definition: it is non-conception. It is wholesome; within it, all things operate dependently, holistically. There is no *I* to create separation. It is unstained, for the store consciousness that colors the way we see and drives the things we do that harm ourselves and others is empty. It is constant: time, coming and going, permanence and impermanence are merely conceptions. The universe is not concerned with our ideas of past, present, or future. As it says in the *Dhammapada*, "If you wish to reach the other shore of existence, give up what is before, behind, and in between. Set your mind free and go beyond birth and death." Let the mind rest here, for this constant realm is not somewhere else; it is the mind in repose in projection only.

You can allow the mind to rest in this realm through a commitment to meditation practice and kind action, but it is also true that the mind is already resting on the foundation of projection only. You are not in some other realm. Vasubandhu is talking about the realm you are in right now. Have a look around.

In the last line of this work, Vasubandhu refers to the Mahayana concepts of three bodies of Buddha: the manifestation body, the bliss body, and the Dharma body. In Sanskrit, these are known as *nirmanakaya*, *sambhogakaya*, and *dharmakaya*, respectively. In simplest terms the manifestation body refers to the physical, historical body of Siddhartha Gautama Buddha; the bliss body refers to the groundless bliss of liberation; and the Dharma body refers to nondualism, limitlessness. In Mahayana Buddhism we think of Buddha's enlightenment as being the realization of the emptiness of all phenomena, of the complete nondualism of everything. Since nothing is separate from Buddha, this was his realization: everything is Buddha. When my teacher stunned my young, troubled, and new-to-Buddhism self by saying "you are Buddha" all those years ago, she was using a teaching based on the idea of the dharmakaya. Nothing is other than Buddha; that is what makes it Buddha. It is not something else—it's just this. The bliss body, sambhogakaya, is the bliss of this realization, which is not attached to any phenomena, outcome, or personal self. I have seen more than one Zen teacher gesturing with their hands as though miming a fountain of joyful energy sweeping through and around their bodies, at a loss for words to describe this blissful body of liberation. Vasubandhu says that realization is this bliss body and this infinite Dharma body.

This work has been laden with complex concepts and models for understanding, and it constantly reminded us that they are only concepts, that they are not the Truth or ultimately real. But now, at the end of this work, Vasubandhu brings us back to the ground of practice—this body, right now. The root of the Buddha's teachings on meditation is mindfulness of the body, and in the *Rohitassa Sutra* he declares, "It is just within this fathom-long body, with its perception and intellect, that I declare that there is the cosmos, the origination of the cosmos, the cessation of the cosmos, and the path of practice leading to the cessation of the cosmos." It is only here in the posture of our spine and the rumblings in our belly that there is a world and an inconceivable, nonself, non-other realm. It is here in the way we walk this path. It is in the way we take care of our body and the way our body takes care of our loved ones and our planet that there is a path to liberation. We can attend to our breathing at any moment to draw ourselves to intimacy with this ground of practice. We can slow down just a bit when we want to rush and strain to get ahead. We can stop and be intimate with how this body is right now, tense and straining, or calm and at rest. We may find that this body is ultimately beyond our understanding, but it is our place to do our best, to manifest our deepest altruistic intentions, to give ourselves. It is the Dharma, the Buddha, the world.

Epilogue:

Meditation and Compassionate Action, and the "Thirty Verses"

There are four principal modes of practice suggested by this text: developing awareness of the power of the storehouse, mindfulness of phenomena, developing awareness of the dependent nature of things, and non-dual meditation. The first two are associated closely with the material in the first half of the "Thirty Verses," the second two with the latter half. The first two are designed to help us let go of afflictive emotions, the second to help us let go of delusion: the delusion that there is a world out there that is separate from us, and an *I* in here that is on its own. They are practices that help us be at peace and realize connection. They operate in close harmony with one another and they can help us to work in close harmony with everything and everyone we encounter.

The power of the store consciousness is vast. This text teaches that we can't directly know what conditions come together to form this moment of consciousness. As it says early on, what the storehouse holds, what karmic seeds are there, is unknown. Modern psychological processes that allow us to dig into the past and analyze, understand, and be free from habits formed in our earlier life can be powerful and transformative. I highly recommend them. However, this is not the method Vasubandhu gives us with this central Yogacara practice of developing awareness of the power of the storehouse. Instead, this text suggests two methods: first, use the mind to understand and recall the vast and complete unknowability of the degree to which what we experience in each moment is conditioned by our past, and second, simply be aware in the moment of what arises in mind. Reading this book, or many parts of it, has been an example of the first aspect of this practice. In his book *Training in Compassion*, Norman Fischer says that we should set out on the Buddhist path by developing a sense of the "awesome power of our karma." In the *Nidana Samyutta* Buddha says: "This body does not belong to you, nor anyone else. It should be regarded as the results of former action [karma] that has been constructed and intended, and is now to be experienced." One way to develop this view is to remind yourself now and again that whatever is here in the present moment, life, is not yours or someone else's. It is conditioning manifesting itself.

Early Buddhist teachings on the subject of karma—and Vasubandhu's here—bring a message of radical empowerment. What arrives in each moment is the result of the past, but in every single instant you have the capacity to create beneficial intention, which will create more harmonious moments in the future. Countless unfathomable things are out of your control, but you always have the opportunity to give your best intention at this moment and thus plant seeds of happiness, kindness, and well-being for all things. Knowing the awesome power of the store consciousness, and knowing our tiny momentary opportunity to participate in this great unfolding, we can be humbled, ennobled, and inspired to do our best. You may not be able to solve homelessness, but you can smile at a disheveled man on the street. You may not be able to eradicate racial injustice, but you can listen to people of color, you can walk to the voting booth, or you can walk hand in hand with the disenfranchised at a civil rights protest. You can't make your colicky baby stop crying, but you can do your best to stay present with how she is and how you are right now.

The second way of practice suggested by the "Thirty Verses," mindfulness of phenomena, is also a way of developing awareness of the power of the store consciousness, but it has countless other merits. If we are aware of what is arising in the present moment without judging, especially if we are aware of the factors Vasubandhu instructs us to attend to, we will begin to see that our thoughts and emotions just seem to appear and disappear. They are not who we are, and they are not so solid and real as we once thought. We can see that the great drama of our lives is actually just a story constructed out of momentary phenomena whose origins we can't ultimately know, but which are deeply rooted in our unconscious, the store consciousness. Many are the times I've been all worked up about some slight I received at work and then found myself seeing the power of the story and the emotions unraveling in the light of mindfulness as I sat cross-legged, quiet, and still in the meditation hall.

This text recommends various mindfulness practices. I will briefly review them here and then give simple instructions on how to bring these practices into your life without being overwhelmed, for they can seem complex.

It is good to begin by developing awareness of the body and the breath. This is the basis of all mindfulness practice taught by the Buddha, and it has been proven over thousands of years in many cultures and traditions to be very effective at helping to stabilize the mind and emotions. Vasubandhu does not make explicit the importance of the body as the basis of mindfulness, but since mindfulness of body through the breath is so central to mindfulness practice in the Buddhist teachings Vasubandhu studied, it is implied that this is where we begin. When we are mindful of sensation in the body, we are mindful of sense-contact, the first universal factor, and when we are attuned to the tension, ease, and rhythm of our breathing, we become more intimate with ourselves, and awareness of emotional states, the second mindfulness practice, may naturally arise.

Vasubandhu is explicit about the importance of mindfulness of the universal and beneficial factors, and of the afflictions and secondary afflictions. Mindfulness of the universal factors requires some study, as they are subtle, and you may want to review chapters 4, 9, and 10. To be mindful of the beneficial and afflictive factors is extremely powerful and can be done intuitively by directing our attention to how we feel, to the condition of our hearts. This kind of awareness both lets our afflictive karma exhaust itself and allows us to refrain from creating more of the same. When we actually intimately know that there is envy in our mind, we can be free of the need to say something sarcastic, rather than impulsively speaking. When we are mindful of tranquility we may enjoy the peace in our hearts, but still step up and get to work.

I am aware that most of the readers of this book will not memorize all fifty-five elements in Vasubandhu's list of mental factors. Even fewer will spend hours of meditation practice silently naming them as they arise. The good news is that we can very effectively work with Vasubandhu's teachings on the power of mindfulness of phenomena anyway. The most important thing is to cultivate a sense of which factors are beneficial and which are harmful and use meditation and simple attentiveness in day-to-day life to develop awareness of which type of body- and mind-states are arising. You may want to compose your own list based on the afflictions you are most likely to experience—fear, helplessness, rage, shame. We all have our individual tendencies. Become intimate with your suffering and your joy. When you are seated on your meditation cushion you don't need to name or control the emotional state; instead, just notice it. When you are at work, consumed with trying to get things to go your way, stop and notice how you feel. Spend some time noticing: take a break, maybe three breaths long, maybe an hour. At home as you prepare for dinner, pause to take stock of how you feel. You can do this any time. For many people it helps to have a plan for when to check in. When you wake up and before sleep are good. You don't need to make, fix, judge, or control when you practice mindfulness of afflictive or beneficial mental factors; you can just stop and be intimate with them, be intimate with yourself, your own beating heart. You can plant seeds of presence, peace, and nonviolence in the ground of the store consciousness.

Let's move on to the third practice suggested by the "Thirty Verses": developing awareness of the dependent nature of phenomena. We sometimes say that complete realization is to see the dependent nature of things without conception, but thinking about, conceptualizing, the dependent nature of things is actually very helpful. When your spouse is standing before you with flushed cheeks and a tense, defensive stance, and your words are coming fast and unwilled, or aggressive silence is thickening in the room, stop to recall that infinite conditions come together to bring him or her to this point of suffering. It's not about you. When you stop to look out across a patch of flowers in a neighbor's yard, think of all the gentle effort made by your neighbor to make this tiny patch of beauty, think of all the ants and worms who lived and died therein, think of the vast, incomprehensible power of the sun that feeds it all, and the fact that each individual raindrop had its place in bringing this moment of you and flowers into being. Let your mind help you to step into a life that sees all things as an infinite web of connection.

The fourth method suggested by this text, nondual meditation practice, is a gateway into intimately realizing that we are always already an expression of the vast web of connection that is the world. The language of nondual meditation can help us soften our minds as we sit and attend to posture and breath. There is no way to sum up what it means to do nondual meditation practice, but various texts provide pointers. Attending to the sensations of the breath in the body is often given as a basic instruction; letting go of all judgment, analysis, and goals gets us on the right track; but ultimately the practice is ungraspable. Nondualism is, by definition, inconceivable. The *Samdhinirmocana Sutra* says, "concentrate on a nonconceptual object." Just rest in just this. Sit without trying to do something or make something happen. Just sit. No need to add anything extra. Give up the operations of mind. Let go of letting go. There is nothing to attain. You do not need to make some special state of mind. Practice is always already realization.

These practices and all the teachings in this book are intended to serve one central purpose, to promote the well-being of everything. Early Buddhist teachings point toward the cessation of suffering, Mahayana toward the liberation of all beings. If we let the focus of the discriminating mind soften, and let semantics aside, we can see a deep and common theme. It may seem that the teachings in the "Thirty Verses" put a great deal of focus on working with the way our consciousness functions, but this is only because our capacity to contribute to the wellness of all things can most truly be realized and liberated, if we know, see through, and shed the unconscious habits that hold us back.

Acknowledgments

Innumerable labors by people I will never know have brought me the opportunity to write this book; infinite conditions arrive to create my desire to say thank you. Many thanks to Weijen Teng, a wonderful partner, buoyant and insightful, in translating the "Thirty Verses." I owe a great debt to many scholars of Yogacara: Stefan Anacker, Jonathan Gold, Thomas Kochumuttom, Dan Lusthaus, Reb Anderson, Thomas Cleary, Thich Nhat Hanh, Tagawa Shun'ei, Charles Muller, Lati Rinbochay, and Red Pine are foremost in my mind. To Taigen Dan Leighton for helping me set my feet on the writing path. The inspiration and support of my teacher Tim Burkett has been constant; little did he know when he decided to host a study group on Yogacara a dozen years ago that a book would emerge. To all my friends on the path at MZMC—in particular Kimberly Johnson, Ted O'Toole, Guy Gibbon, Rosemary Taylor, Susan Nelson, Wanda Isle, and Stacy Lee King—a bow. To all the many dear friends around the world who are so supportive as I wander down the paths the muse inspires, thanks! To Laura Cunningham and all the other great folks at Wisdom

Publications: I love working with you guys, thank you! To Bussho Martin Lahn, a true friend on the path, I offer a question: Is there gratitude when there is no other?

To all the teachers of yoga, all the therapists and psychologists, the chemical dependency counselors, the friends of Bill W., who have helped this stream of consciousness run more and more clear and free, thanks so much! To David and Christine at the Colfax Abbey. To the many great figures of the Buddhist tradition; to Buddha, Dharma, and Sangha; to those who have touched my own heart the most across vast space, time, and culture: Gotama Buddha, Mahapajapati, Patacara, Vasubandhu, Shitou, Xinggang, Dogen; to zazen, just this, just this—great gratitude!

To my mom, my dad, my brother: there is no me without you. For my dear Colleen, much love. For Finn, Daisy, and Delaney, thanks for letting me in! For my boys Rocky and Max, you are my greatest inspiration.

To you, dear reader, thank you, with all my heart, for your practice.

Selected Bibliography

Anacker, Stefan. *Seven Works of Vasubandhu*. Delhi: Motilal Banarsidass, 1984.

Anderson, Reb. *The Third Turning of the Wheel*. Berkeley: Rodmell Press, 2012.

Bodhi, Bhikku. *In the Buddha's Words*. Boston: Wisdom Publications, 2005.

———. *The Connected Discourses of the Buddha*. Boston: Wisdom Publications, 2000.

———. *The Middle Length Discourses of the Buddha*. Boston: Wisdom Publications, 1995.

Caplow, Florence, and Susan Moon. *The Hidden Lamp*. Boston: Wisdom Publications, 2013.

Cleary, Thomas. *Buddhist Yoga*. Boston: Shambhala Publications, 1995.

Cook, Francis. *Three Texts on Consciousness Only*. Moraga, CA: BDK, 2006.

Easwaran, Eknath. *The Dhammapada*. Tomales, CA: Nilgiri Press, 1985.

Gold, Jonathan. *Paving the Great Way*. New York: Columbia University Press, 2014.

Guenther, Herbert, and Leslie Kawamura. *The Necklace of Pure Understanding*. Emeryville, CA: Dharma Publishing, 1975.

Hanh, Thich Nhat. *Buddha Mind, Buddha Body*. Berkeley: Parallax, 2007.

———. *Understanding Our Mind*. Berkeley: Parallax, 2006.

Hakeda, Yoshito. *The Awakening of Faith*. New York: Columbia University Press, 1967.

Hopkins, Jeffery. *Emptiness in the Mind Only School of Buddhism*. Berkeley: University of California Press, 2003.

Kochumuttom, Thomas A. *A Buddhist Doctrine of Experience*. Delhi: Motilal Banarsidass, 1982.

Lusthaus, Dan. *Buddhist Phenomenology*. New York: RoutledgeCurzon, 1992.

Murcott, Susan. *The First Buddhist Women*. Berkeley: Parallax, 1991.

Okumura, Shohaku. *Realizing Genjokoan*. Boston: Wisdom Publications, 2010.

Pine, Red. *The Lankavatara Sutra*. Berkeley: Counterpoint, 2012.

Rinbochay, Lati. *Mind in Tibetan Buddhism*. Valois, NY: Snow Lion, 1980.

Shun'ei, Tagawa. *Living Yogacara*. Boston: Wisdom Publications, 2009.

Waldron, William. *The Buddhist Unconscious*. Abingdon UK: Routledge, 2003.

Willis, Janice Dean. *On Knowing Reality*. New York: Columbia University Press, 1982

The "Thirty Verses" in Devanagari and Romanized Script

अथ त्रिंशिकाविज्ञप्तिकारिकाः
atha triṃśikāvijñaptikārikāḥ

आत्मधर्मोपचारो हि विविधो यः प्रवर्तते ।
विज्ञानपरिणामेऽसौ परिणामः स च त्रिधा ॥ १ ॥
ātmadharmopacāro hi vividho yaḥ pravartate |
vijñānapariṇāme 'sau pariṇāmaḥ sa ca tridhā || 1 ||

विपाको मननाख्यश्च विज्ञप्तिर्विषयस्य च ।
तत्रालयाख्यं विज्ञानं विपाकः सर्वबीजकम् ॥ २ ॥
vipāko mananākhyaś ca vijñaptir viṣayasya ca |
tatrālayākhyaṃ vijñānaṃ vipākaḥ sarvabījakam || 2 ||

असंविदितकोपादिस्थानविज्ञप्तिकं च तत् ।
सदा स्पर्शमनस्कारवित्संज्ञाचेतनान्वितम् ॥ ३ ॥
asaṃviditakopādisthānavijñaptikaṃ ca tat |
sadā sparśamanaskāravitsañjñācetanānvitam || 3 ||

उपेक्षा वेदना तत्रानिवृताव्याकृतं च तत् ।
तथा स्पर्शादयस्तच्च वर्तते स्रोतसौघवत् ॥ ४ ॥
upekṣā vedanā tatrānivṛtāvyākṛtaṃ ca tat |
tathā sparśādayas tac ca vartate srotasaughavat || 4 ||

तस्य व्यावृत्तिरर्हत्त्वे तदाश्रित्य प्रवर्तते ।
तदालम्बं मनोनाम विज्ञानं मननात्मकम् ॥ ५ ॥

tasya vyāvṛtir arhatve tadāśritya pravartate |
tadālambaṃ manonāma vijñānaṃ mananātmakam || 5 ||

क्लेशैश्चतुर्भिः सहितं निवृताव्याकृतैः सदा ।
आत्मदृष्ट्यात्ममोहात्ममानात्मस्नेहसंज्ञितैः ॥ ६ ॥

kleśaiś caturbhiḥ sahitaṃ nivṛtāvyākṛtaiḥ sadā |
ātmadṛṣṭyātmamohātmamānātmasnehasañjñitaiḥ || 6 ||

यत्रजस्तन्मयैरन्यैः स्पर्शाद्यैश्चार्हतो न तत् ।
न निरोधसमापत्तौ मार्गे लोकोत्तरे न च ॥ ७ ॥

yatrajas tanmayair anyaiḥ sparśādyaiś cārhato na tat |
na nirodhasamāpattau mārge lokottare na ca || 7 ||

द्वितीयः परिणामोऽयं तृतीयः षड्विधस्य या ।
विषयस्योपलब्धिः सा कुशलाकुशलाद्वया ॥ ८ ॥

dvitīyaḥ pariṇāmo 'yaṃ tṛtīyaḥ ṣaḍvidhasya yā |
viṣayasyopalabdhiḥ sā kuśalākuśalādvayā || 8 ||

सर्वत्रगैर्विनियतैः कुशलैश्चैतसैरसौ ।
सम्प्रयुक्ता तथा क्लेशैरुपक्लेशैस्त्रिवेदना ॥ ९ ॥

sarvatragair viniyataiḥ kuśalaiś caitasair asau |
samprayuktā tathā kleśair upakleśais trivedanā || 9 ||

आद्याः स्पर्शादयश्छन्दाधिमोक्षस्मृतयः सह ।
समाधिधीभ्यां नियताः श्रद्धाथ ह्रीरपत्रपा ॥ १० ॥

ādyāḥ sparśādayaś chandādhimokṣasmṛtayaḥ saha |
samādhidhībhyāṃ niyatāḥ śraddhātha hrīrapatrapā || 10 ||

अलोभादित्रयं वीर्यं प्रश्रब्धिः साप्रमादिका ।
अहिंसा कुशलाः क्लेशा रागप्रतिघमूढयः ॥ ११ ॥

alobhādi trayaṃ vīryaṃ praśrabdhiḥ sāpramādikā |
ahiṃsā kuśalāḥ kleśā rāgapratighamūḍhayaḥ || 11 ||

मानदृग्विचिकित्साश्च क्रोधोपनहने पुनः ।
म्रक्षः प्रदाश ईर्ष्याथ मात्सर्यं सह मायया ॥ १२ ॥

mānadṛgvicikitsāś ca krodhopanahane punaḥ |
mrakṣaḥ pradāśa īrṣyātha mātsaryaṃ saha māyayā || 12 ||

शाठ्यं मदोऽविहिंसा ह्रीरत्रपा स्त्यानमुद्धवः ।
आश्रद्ध्यमथ कौसीद्यं प्रमादो मुषिता स्मृतिः ॥ १३ ॥

śāṭhyaṃ mado vihiṃsāhrīratrapā styānam uddhavaḥ |
āśraddham atha kausīdyaṃ pramādo muṣitā smṛtiḥ || 13 ||

विक्षेपोऽसम्प्रजन्यं च कौकृत्यं मिद्धमेव च ।
वितर्कश्च विचारश्चेत्युपक्लेशा द्वये द्विधा ॥ १४ ॥

vikṣepo 'samprajanyaṃ ca kaukṛtyaṃ middham eva ca |
vitarkaś ca vicāraś cety upakleśā dvaye dvidhā || 14 ||

पञ्चानां मूलविज्ञाने यथाप्रत्ययमुद्भवः ।
विज्ञानानां सह न वा तरङ्गाणां यथा जले ॥ १५ ॥

pañcānāṃ mūlavijñāne yathāpratyayam udbhavaḥ |
vijñānānāṃ saha na vā taraṅgāṇāṃ yathā jale || 15 ||

मनोविज्ञानसंभूतिः सर्वदासंज्ञिकादृते ।
समापत्तिद्वयान्मिद्धान्मूर्च्छनादप्यचित्तकात् ॥ १६ ॥

manovijñānasambhūtiḥ sarvadāsañjñikād ṛte |
samāpattidvayān middhān mūrchanād apy acittakāt || 16 ||

विज्ञानपरिणामोऽयं विकल्पो यद् विकल्प्यते ।
तेन तन्नास्ति तेनेदं सर्वं विज्ञप्तिमात्रकम् ॥१७॥

vijñānapariṇāmo 'yaṃ vikalpo yad vikalpyate |
tena tan nāsti tenedaṃ sarvaṃ vijñaptimātrakam || 17 ||

सर्वबीजं हि विज्ञानं परिणामस्तथा तथा ।
यात्यन्योऽन्यवशाद् येन विकल्पः स स जायते ॥१८॥

sarvabījaṃ hi vijñānaṃ pariṇāmas tathā tathā |
yāty anyonyavaśād yena vikalpaḥ sa sa jāyate || 18 ||

कर्मणो वासना ग्राहद्वयवासनया सह ।
क्षीणे पूर्वविपाकेऽन्यद् विपाकं जनयन्ति तत् ॥१९॥

karmaṇo vāsanā grāhadvayavāsanayā saha |
kṣīṇe pūrvavipāke 'nyadvipākaṃ janayanti tat || 19 ||

येन येन विकल्पेन यद् यद् वस्तु विकल्प्यते ।
परिकल्पित एवासौ स्वभावो न स विद्यते ॥२०॥

yena yena vikalpena yad yad vastu vikalpyate |
parikalpita evāsau svabhāvo na sa vidyate || 20 ||

परतन्त्रस्वभावस्तु विकल्पः प्रत्ययोद्भवः ।
निष्पन्नस्तस्य पूर्वेण सदा रहितता तु या ॥२१॥

paratantrasvabhāvas tu vikalpaḥ pratyayodbhavaḥ |
niṣpannas tasya pūrveṇa sadā rahitatā tu yā || 21 ||

अत एव स नैवान्यो नानन्यः परतन्त्रतः ।
अनित्यतादिवद् वाच्यो नादृष्टेऽस्मिन् स दृश्यते ॥२२॥

ata eva sa naivānyo nānanyaḥ paratantrataḥ |
anityatādivad vācyo nādṛṣṭe 'smin sa dṛśyate || 22 ||

त्रिविधस्य स्वभावस्य त्रिविधां निःस्वभावताम्।
सन्धाय सर्वधर्माणां देशिता निःस्वभावता॥२३॥

trividhasya svabhāvasya trividhāṃ niḥsvabhāvatām |
sandhāya sarvadharmāṇāṃ deśitā niḥsvabhāvatā || 23 ||

प्रथमो लक्षणेनैव निःस्वभावोऽपरः पुनः।
न स्वयंभाव एतस्येत्यपरा निःस्वभावता॥२४॥

prathamo lakṣaṇenaiva niḥsvabhāvo 'paraḥ punaḥ |
na svayambhāva etasyety aparā niḥsvabhāvatā || 24 ||

धर्माणां परमार्थश्च स यतस्तथताऽपि सः।
सर्वकालं तथाभावात् सैव विज्ञप्तिमात्रता॥२५॥

dharmāṇāṃ paramārthaś ca sa yatas tathatāpi saḥ |
sarvakālaṃ tathābhāvāt saiva vijñaptimātratā || 25 ||

यावद् विज्ञप्तिमात्रत्वे विज्ञानं नावतिष्ठति।
ग्राहद्वयस्यानुशयस्तावन्न विनिवर्तते॥२६॥

yāvad vijñaptimātratve vijñānaṃ nāvatiṣṭhati |
grāhadvayasyānuśayastāvan na vinivartate || 26 ||

विज्ञप्तिमात्रमेवेदमित्यपि ह्युपलम्भतः।
स्थापयन्नग्रतः किञ्चित् तन्मात्रे नावतिष्ठते॥२७॥

vijñaptimātram evedam ity api hay upalambhataḥ |
sthāpayann agrataḥ kiñcit tanmātre nāvatiṣṭhate || 27 ||

यदालम्बनं ज्ञानं नैवोपलभते तदा।
स्थितं विज्ञानमात्रत्वे ग्राह्याभावे तदग्रहात्॥२८॥

yadālambanaṃ vijñānaṃ naivopalabhate tadā |
sthitaṃ vijñānamātratve grāhyābhāve tadagrahāt || 28 ||

अचित्तोऽनुपलम्भोऽसौ ज्ञानं लोकोत्तरं च तत् ।
आश्रयस्य परावृत्तिर्द्विधा दौष्ठुल्यहानितः ॥२९॥

acitto 'nupalambho 'sau jñānaṃ lokottaraṃ ca tat |
āśrayasya parāvṛttir dvidhā dauṣṭhulyahānitaḥ || 29 ||

स एवानास्रवो धातुरचिन्त्यः कुशलो ध्रुवः ।
सुखो विमुक्तिकायोऽसौ धर्माख्योऽयं महामुनेः ॥३०॥

sa evānasravo dhātur acintyaḥ kuśalo dhruvaḥ |
sukho vimuktikāyo 'sau dharmākhyo 'yaṃ mahāmuneḥ || 30 ||

॥लिंशिकाविज्ञप्तिकारिकाः समाप्ताः ॥
triṃśikāvijñaptikārikāḥ samāptāḥ

English-to-Sanskrit Glossary

affliction	*kleśa*
aggregate	*skandha*
beneficial	*kuśala*
complete, realized nature	*(pari)niṣpanna svabhāva*
conceptualization	*vikalpa*
consciousness of self	*manas*
consciousness	*vijñāna*
dharma body	*dharmakāya*
form	*rūpa*
formation	*saṃskāra*
grasping self and other	*grāha dvaya*
harmful	*akuśala*
imaginary nature	*parikalpita svabhāva*
meditation of cessation	*nirodha samāpatti*
no-self nature	*niḥsvabhāvatā*
other-dependent nature	*paratantra svabhāva*
overturned at root	*āśraya parāvṛtti*
projection only	*vijñapti mātra*
projection	*vijñapti*
ripening	*vipāka*
root consciousness	*mūla vijñāna*
seed	*bīja*
store(house) consciousness	*ālaya vijñāna*

supramundane awareness	*jñāna lokottara*
thought consciousness	*manovijñāna*
three feelings	*trivedanā*
thusness	*tathatā*
transformation	*pariṇāma*

Universal Factors

sense contact	*sparśa*
attention	*manaskāra*
sensation	*vedanā*
perception	*saṃjñā*
volition	*cetanā*

Four Afflictions Associated with Manas

self view	*ātma dṛṣṭi*
self delusion	*ātma moha*
self pride	*ātma māna*
self love	*ātma sneha*

Specific Factors

aspiration	*chanda*
resolve	*adhimokṣa*
memory	*smṛti*
concentration	*samādhi*
intellection	*prajñā/dhibhyam*

Beneficial Factors

faith	*śraddhā*
conscience	*hrī*
humility	*apatrāpya*
nonattachment	*alobha*

nonhatred	*adveṣa*
nondelusion	*amoha*
energy	*vīrya*
tranquility	*praśrabdhi*
carefulness	*apramāda*
equanimity	*upekṣā*
nonviolence	*ahiṃsā*

Afflictions

desire	*rāga*
aversion	*pratigha*
delusion	*moha*
pride	*māna*
wrong view	*mithyā dṛṣṭi*
doubt	*vicikitsā*

Secondary Afflictions

anger	*krodha*
hatred	*upanāha*
hypocrisy	*mrakṣa*
malice	*pradāśa*
envy	*īrṣyā*
selfishness	*mātsarya*
deceitfulness	*māyā*
guile	*śāṭhya*
arrogance	*mada*
harmfulness	*vihiṃsā*
lack of conscience	*āhrīkya*
lack of humility	*anapatrāpya*
sluggishness	*styāna*
restlessness	*auddhatya*

lack of faith	*āśraddhya*
laziness	*pramāda*
carelessness	*kausīdya*
forgetfulness	*muṣitasmṛti*
distraction	*vikṣepa*
unawareness	*samprajñā*

Indeterminate Factors

remorse	*kaukṛtya*
sleepiness	*middha*
initial thought	*vitarka*
analysis	*vicāra*

Index

as fifth aggregate, 50
mano as, 115, 117
of mindfulness, 93
storehouse and, 90–91, 110
without object, 187, 188–90
See also thought consciousness
koans, 87
Kuan Yin, 87–88

L
labeling, 85–86
Lankavatara Sutra, 3, 4, 109–10
liberation
  from conditioning, 133
  as end of twofold grasping,
    134–36
  meditation and, 71
  as no-thing, 152
  three marks and, 154
  three natures and, 137
  views of, 6–7, 18, 175
  See also blissful body of libera-
    tion (*sambhogakaya*); nirvana
loving-kindness meditation, 104

M
Mahayana Buddhism
  Abhidharma and, 28–29, 123
  consciousness in, 182–83
  Consciousness Only and,
    10–11
  Early Buddhism and, 6–7, 123
  emphasis of, 18, 30, 135, 157,
    168
  nirvana in, 71–72, 173, 175

nondualism in, 151–52
not existing, understanding of
  in, 122–23
overview of, 6–7
three bodies of Buddha in, 193
three natures and, 8
transcending conceptualization in, 145
two truths in, 137–38
Vasubandhu's role in, 2
wrong view in, 107
Yogacara and, 3–4, 145,
  155–56
manas, 20
  as basic aspect of conscious-
    ness, 61
  birth and development of, 20,
    58–60, 69–70
  in deep meditation, 71–72
  enlightenment and, 184, 189
  five universal factors and, 87,
    88
  four afflictions and, 63, 64–66
  as obstructed but neutral,
    67–68
  role of, 33, 34–35, 57, 70,
    129–30, 132–33
  as sense base, 116
  suffering and, 63
  supramundane awareness
    and, 188
Mazu, 181
meditation
  of cessation, 20, 69, 70, 71
  commitment to, 17, 192

thought consciousness and, 21,
115, 117
Universal Recommendation for Zazen
(Dogen), 159, 161

V
Vasubandhu
  and Abhidharma, relationship
    to, 6, 108
  ability to find common
    ground, 71, 72, 173–74
  ethics, view of, 96–97
  fundamental problem accord-
    ing to, 135–36
  other-dependent nature,
    approach to, 145
  role in Buddhism, 1, 2–3, 7,
    17–18
  vijnapti-matra, use of, 32–33, 124
vipassana (insight), 158, 159–61
Vipassana tradition, 5, 74
volition
  manas and, 69, 88
  as mental factor, 19, 20, 49,
    52–53, 69, 85
  mindfulness of, 76, 86–87

W
wellness and well-being
  beneficial factors and, 90–91,
    92–93
  caring for mental states as, 77
  commitment to, 105–6, 202
  opening to, 64
  right effort and, 79

transforming consciousness
  for, 82
wisdom of equality, 67–68
wrong view, 107, 151–52

X
Xuanzang, 127. See also
  Chengweishilun

Y
Yaoshan, 148–49, 161
yoga, uses of term, 3
Yogacara
  approach in this book, 18
  Consciousness Only and, 9
  critiques of, 155–56
  enlightenment in, 181
  manas in, 57, 61
  other Buddhist schools and,
    29–30
  overview of, 3–4
  phenomena in. *See* three natures
  suffering, view of in, 70–71, 132
  Vasubandhu's role in, 2
Yogacarabhumi (Asanga), 45, 59

Z
Zen
  Consciousness Only in, 9–10
  five universals, appearance of
    in, 87
  meditation in, 74
  precepts in, 97
  right effort in, 80
  Yogacara in, 4, 18

About the Author and Translator

BEN CONNELLY is a Soto Zen teacher and Dharma heir in the Katagiri lineage. He is also a professional musician and teaches mindfulness in many secular contexts including police and corporate training, correctional facilities, and addiction recovery groups. Ben is based at Minnesota Zen Meditation Center and travels to teach across the United States. He lives in Minneapolis, Minnesota.

WEIJEN TENG is an assistant professor at Dharma Drum University in Taiwan. He has a BA in Pali and Buddhist studies (Kelaniya, Sri Lanka), MA in Sanskrit (Poona, India), and PhD in religious studies (Harvard University). His particular areas of research include Abhidharma and Yogacara meditation theories, study in Chinese translation of Sanskrit texts, and development of contemporary Chinese Buddhism.

What to Read Next
from Wisdom Publications

INSIDE THE GRASS HUT
Living Shitou's Classic Zen Poem
Ben Connelly
Foreword by Taigen Dan Leighton

"The very essence of Zen."
—Mike O'Connor

LIVING YOGACARA
An Introduction to Consciousness-Only Buddhism
Tagawa Shun'ei
Translated and Introduced by Charles Muller

"This book, expertly translated by Charles Muller, is exceptional for making an extremely complex tradition accessible to the general reader."
—*Buddhadharma*

AN INTELLIGENT LIFE
Buddhist Psychology of Self-Transformation
Koitsu Yokoyama

"This welcome new voice in American publishing demonstrates with sparkling clarity how Buddhist wisdom can address life's most pressing questions."
—*Publishers Weekly*

About Wisdom Publications

Wisdom Publications is the leading publisher of classic and contemporary Buddhist books and practical works on mindfulness. To learn more about us or to explore our other books, please visit our website at wisdompubs.org or contact us at the address below.

Wisdom Publications
199 Elm Street
Somerville, MA 02144 USA

We are a 501(c)(3) organization, and donations in support of our mission are tax deductible.

Wisdom Publications is affiliated with the Foundation for the Preservation of the Mahayana Tradition (FPMT).